Charles Dickens

Hard Times

Adapted for the stage by Deborah McAndrew

Bloomsbury Methuen Drama
An imprint of Bloomsbury Publishing Plc

B L O O M S B U R Y
LONDON · OXFORD · NEW YORK · NEW DELHI · SYDNEY

Bloomsbury Methuen Drama

An imprint of Bloomsbury Publishing Plc

Imprint previously known as Methuen Drama

50 Bedford Square	1385 Broadway
London	New York
WC1B 3DP	NY 10018
UK	USA

www.bloomsbury.com

**BLOOMSBURY, METHUEN DRAMA and the Diana logo
are trademarks of Bloomsbury Publishing Plc**

First published 2018

British Library Cataloguing-in-Publication Data
A catalogue record for this book is available from the British Library.

ISBN: PB: 978-1-3500-8310-3
ePDF: 978-1-3500-8311-0
eBook: 9978-1-3500-8312-7

Series: Modern Plays

Front cover design by Anonymous Design

Typeset by Mark Heslington Ltd, Scarborough, North Yorkshire

To find out more about our authors and books visit *www.bloomsbury.com*.
Here you will find extracts, author interviews, details of forthcoming
events and the option to sign up for our *newsletters*.

HARD TIMES

By Charles Dickens

Adapted for the stage by Deborah McAndrew

CAST

Vanessa Schofield	Louisa Gradgrind / Fire-eater
Perry Moore	Tom Gradgrind / Juggler
Suzanne Ahmet	Sissy Jupe
Andrew Price	Thomas Gradgrind / Union Chairman / Clown
Howard Chadwick	Josiah Bounderby / Strong Man
Victoria Brazier	Mrs Sparsit / Rachael / Miss Josephine Sleary
Anthony Hunt	Steven Blackpool / The Wild Huntsman
Darren Kuppan	Mr Harthouse / Bitzer / Cupid / Mill Hand
Claire Storey	Mrs Gradgrind / Mrs Pegler / Snake-charmer
Paul Barnhill	Mr Sleary / Mr Slackbridge / Mill Hand

Director & Composer	Conrad Nelson
Designer	Dawn Allsopp
Lighting Designer	Mark Howland
Musical Director	Rebekah Hughes
Choreographer	Beverley Norris-Edmunds
Production Manager	Kay Packwood
Company Stage Manager	Megan Sheeran
Deputy Stage Manager	Jay Hirst
Technical Manager	Symon Culpan
Costume Supervisor	Lucy Archbould
Costumes made by	Lucy Archbould
and Wardrobe Interns	Sarah Lillie Rose and Sarah-Jayne Bell
Education	Deborah McAndrew
Production Photographer	Nobby Clark
Marketing	The Experience Business
Press & PR	Duncan Clarke PR
Executive Director	Sue Andrews
Finance Officer	Katie English

Produced by Northern Broadsides Theatre Company, the first performance of *Hard Times* was at the Viaduct Theatre, Halifax, on 16th February 2018

Hard Times

Characters *(for 10 actors, with suggested doubling)*

Louisa Gradgrind / Fire-eater

Tom Gradgrind / Juggler

Sissy Jupe

Thomas Gradgrind / Union Chairman / Clown

Josiah Bounderby / Strong Man

Mrs Sparsit / Rachael / Miss Josephine Sleary

Steven Blackpool / The Wild Huntsman

Mr Harthouse / Bitzer / Cupid / Mill Hand

Mrs Gradgrind / Mrs Pegler / Snake-charmer

Mr Sleary / Mr Slackbridge / Mill Hand

Prologue

The exterior of a circus tent: flags and banners.

As the audience enter, Circus people promenade and play.

Mr Sleary, *assisted by* **Sissy Jupe**, *welcomes the audience in with chatter and spiel; brandishing tickets and barking for more customers in a lisping voice . . .*

Sleary Hurry ladies. Hurry gentlemen. Hurry children – to see the slack wire, the tight rope, knife-throwers, jugglers, acrobatics – the Human Pyramid – on bareback steeds!

Sissy Hurry – to see Signor Jupe and his highly trained performing dog, Merrylegs!

Sleary Hurry – to see The Wild Huntsman of the North American Prairies perform his daring vaulting act.

Sissy And Signor Jupe's astounding feat of throwing seventy-five hundred-weight in rapid succession backhanded over his head – thus forming a fountain of solid iron in mid-air . . .

Sleary Hurry – for pleasing, but always strictly moral, wonders which must be seen to be believed.

When all area seated the music stops.

Blackout.

Lights up on **Sleary**.

Sleary (*Sings.*)
 When I was just a nipper, on my mother's knee
 I learned about the life that was in store for me
 A noble occupation, and my father's legacy
 To grace this dreary world with a little artistry . . .

 To the edges of the town
 Come the juggler and the clown
 Here the Wild Huntsman will give you a thrill
 Riding and shooting with breathtaking skill

Leave your troubles far behind
And the daily graft and grind
Let the doyen of equestrian arts
Lighten your burden and gladden your hearts

Brave and daring! (*gasp*) Trapeze and wire!
Strength and might, all for your delight.
Fearless, flaring! Rattlesnake and fire!
Run away, run away, run away with us tonight.

When the circus comes around
There is solace to be found
All your vexation, the bills and the rent
Seem to dissolve as you enter the tent

For the happiness you feel
Has the power to help and heal

All   Come and see Sleary, and you can be sure
He has the medicine, he has the cure

La la la, la la, la la . . . (etc . . .)

Sleary (*Spoken.*)   Ah, be sure you see Miss Josephine Sleary, and her Graceful Tyrolean Flower Act

All   Graceful, gliding! (*Bell, whistle, cymbal!*)

Sleary   Bold and bright, all for your delight.

All   Bareback riding! (*Horn, whiz, cymbal!*)
Run away, run away, run away with us tonight.

Sleary *and the Circus performers disappear into the tent, leaving* **Sissy Jupe** *behind.*

Act One

Scene One

Outside Sleary's Horse-riding

Enter **Thomas Gradgrind**, *pausing at a distance.*

Sissy   Hurry sir! The show has already started. Miss Josephine Sleary is inaugurating the entertainments with her graceful Tyrolean flower act. Hurry hurry hurry!

Gradgrind   Flowers? Are these flowers in actuality?

Sissy (*Realising who it is.*)   Actu . . . actu . . .?

Gradgrind   Are they real?

Sissy   No sir, they're silk.

Gradgrind   Girl number twenty, is that you?

Sissy   Yes Mr Gradgrind, sir.

Gradgrind   You are new to my school.

Sissy   Yes sir. My father wishes that I should be educated.

Gradgrind   I very much want girls to join my school. You are girl number twenty.

And what is your name?

Sissy   Sissy, Jupe, sir.

Gradgrind   Sissy is not a name. Don't call yourself Sissy. Call yourself Cecilia.

Sissy   It's father as calls me Sissy, sir.

Gradgrind   Then he has no business to do it. What is your father?

Sissy   He's Signor Jupe! He belongs to the horse-riding. Would you like to see Miss Sleary now, sir, doing her flower act?

Gradgrind   Certainly not. I am a practical man. Do we ever see flowers on horseback in reality – in fact? Do we?

Sissy   No sir.

Gradgrind   No, and you are not to see anywhere what you don't see in fact; you are not to have anywhere what you don't have in fact. What is called Taste is only another name for fact. Tell me, would you use a carpet having a representation of flowers upon it?

Sissy   If you please, sir, I am very fond of flowers.

Gradgrind   And you would put tables and chairs upon them, and have people walking over them with heavy boots?

Sissy   It wouldn't hurt them, sir. They would be the pictures of what is very pretty and pleasant and I would fancy –

Gradgrind   Ay ay ay! But you mustn't fancy, Cecilia Jupe! Fact, fact, fact! This is the principle on which I run my school, and on which I bring up my own children.

Sissy   Your own children, sir?

Gradgrind   My own children have experienced education of the reason. My children settle everything by means of addition, subtraction, multiplication and division, and never wonder.

Sissy   Never, sir?

Gradgrind   Never.

Sleary *suddenly reappears from the tent with* **Louisa** *and* **Tom**.

Sleary   Be off with you, you young rascals – and don't come back without a penny each. Miss Josephine Sleary does not perform for free.

Gradgrind   Louisa! Thomas!

Louisa   Father!

Sleary   Are these yours, Squire? Then I regret to report
that they were caught sneaking under the side of the tent.
Entry fee is just a penny each, Squire – so that'll be
threepence with your good self . . .

Gradgrind   I do not desire entry, sir.

Sleary   Sleary's the name, Squire. As you wish. Sissy, your
father is asking for you.

Sissy *flees into the tent.*

Good afternoon, Squire.

Exit **Sleary** *as* **Gradgrind** *rounds on his children.*

Gradgrind   Louisa! Thomas! In the name of wonder,
idleness and folly, what do you do here?

Louisa   Wanted to see what it was like.

Gradgrind   What it was like?

Louisa   Yes Father.

Gradgrind   Thomas, though I have the fact before me,
I find it difficult to believe that you, with your education
and resources, should have brought your sister to a scene
like this.

Louisa   I brought him, Father. I asked him to come.

Gradgrind   I am sorry to hear it. I am very sorry indeed
to hear it. It makes Thomas no better, and it makes you
worse, Louisa.

Louisa *is impassive.* **Tom** *still won't meet his father's eyes.*

You! To whom the circle of the sciences is open; who may be
said to be replete with facts; who have been trained to
mathematical exactness; Thomas and you, here! In this
degraded situation.

Louisa   I was tired, Father. I have been tired a long time.

Gradgrind   Tired? Of what?

Louisa   I don't know of what – of everything, I think.

Gradgrind   Say not another word. I will hear no more. What would your best friends say, Louisa? Do you attach no value to their good opinion? What would Mr Bounderby say? What would Mr Bounderby say?

In one swift movement, he marches his children away.

Scene Two

The Gradgrinds' Parlour

Mr Bounderby *standing, regaling the seated* **Mrs Gradgrind** *about the hardships of his childhood.*

Bounderby   A ditch, ma'am. I spent my tenth birthday in a ditch. Not that a ditch was new to me, for I was born in a ditch.

Mrs G   I hope it was at least a dry ditch, Mr Bounderby.

Bounderby   No indeed, Mrs Gradgrind! As wet as a sop. A foot of water in it.

Mrs G   Enough to give a baby cold.

Bounderby   Cold? I was born with inflammation of the lungs, and of everything else that was capable of inflammation.

Mrs G   I hope your mother / would have . . .

Bounderby   My mother? Bolted, ma'am. Left me to my grandmother – the wickedest old woman that ever lived. She kept a chandler's shop, and kept me in an egg-box. As soon as I was big enough to run away, I ran away.

Then I became a young vagabond; and instead of one old woman knocking me about and starving me, everybody of all ages knocked me about and starved me. But I pulled through it, Mrs Gradgrind, though nobody threw me out a rope. Vagabond, errand boy, vagabond, labourer, porter, clerk, chief manager, small partner, Josiah Bounderby of Coketown. Those are the antecedents, and the culmination.

Enter **Mr Gradgrind**, *with* **Louisa** *and* **Tom**.

Gradgrind   Bounderby, you're here!

Bounderby   What's the matter, Gradgrind? What is young Thomas in the dumps about? (*Though he speaks of* **Thomas**, *he looks at* **Louisa**.)

Louisa   We sneaked into the circus and Father caught us.

Gradgrind   I should as soon have expected to find my children reading poetry!

Mrs G   Dear me. How can you, Louisa and Thomas! What can you possibly want to know of circuses? I am sure you have enough to do. With my head in its present throbbing state, I couldn't remember half the mere names of half the facts you have got to attend to.

Louisa   That's the reason.

Mrs G   Don't tell me that's the reason, because it can't be nothing of the sort.

Go and be something-ological directly.

Louisa *and* **Tom** *step apart and sit down to read encyclopaedic tomes.*

Gradgrind   Bounderby, you are always so interested in my young people – particularly in Louisa – that I make no apology for saying to you, I am very much vexed by this discovery. I have systematically devoted myself to the education of the reason of my family, and yet it would appear from this unexpected circumstance as if something has crept into Thomas's and Louisa's minds in which their reason has no part.

Bounderby   There certainly is no reason in looking with interest at a parcel of vagabonds. When I was a vagabond myself, nobody looked with any interest at me; I know that.

Gradgrind   Then comes the question; in what has this vulgar curiosity its rise?

Bounderby   In idle imagination, Gradgrind. A very bad thing for anybody, but a cursed bad thing for a girl like Louisa.

Gradgrind   Is it possible that, in spite of all precautions, a story-book can have got into the house? Because, in minds that have been practically formed by rule and line, from the cradle upwards, this is so curious, so incomprehensible.

Bounderby   Stop a bit! You have one of those strollers' children in the school.

Gradgrind   Cecilia Jupe by name.

Bounderby   Now, stop a bit! How did she come there?

Gradgrind   She specially applied here at the house to be admitted, as not regularly belonging to our town.

Bounderby   Now, stop a bit! Louisa saw her when she came?

Gradgrind   Louisa certainly did see her, for she mentioned the application to me.

But saw her, I have no doubt, in Mrs Gradgrind's presence.

Bounderby *and* **Gradgrind** *turn to accuse* **Mrs Gradgrind**.

Mrs G   The girl wanted to come to the school, and Mr Gradgrind wanted girls to come to the school, and Louisa and Thomas both said that the girl wanted to come, and that Mr Gradgrind wanted girls to come, and how was it possible to contradict them when such was the fact? Oh, my poor health!

Exit **Mrs Gradgrind** *– tearfully.*

Bounderby   Now I tell you what, Gradgrind. Turn this girl out of the school, and do it at once. When I thought I would run away from my egg-box and my grandmother, I did it at once. Do you the same.

Gradgrind   Are you walking, Bounderby? Perhaps you wouldn't mind walking back to the circus with me?

Bounderby   Not in the least, Gradgrind – as long as you do it at once!

The men pick up their hats and set out, passing **Louisa** *and* **Tom**. **Bounderby** *pauses . . .*

It's all right now, Louisa; it's all right, young Thomas. I'll answer for it being all over with your father. Well, Louisa, that's worth a kiss, isn't it?

Louisa   You can take one, Mr Bounderby.

Louisa *offers her cheek.* **Bounderby** *kisses.*

Bounderby   Always my pet; ain't you, Louisa?

Exit **Bounderby**.

Louisa *takes out a handkerchief and rubs her face.*

Tom   What are you about, Loo? You'll rub a hole in your face.

Louisa   You may cut the piece out with your penknife if you like, Tom. I wouldn't cry.

Scene Three

Outside Sleary's Horse-riding

Sissy Jupe *comes running, pursued by* **Bitzer**. **Sissy** *carries a bottle of oil.*

Sissy   Leave me alone, Bitzer!

Bitzer   I can help you, girl number twenty.

Sissy   I don't want your help. You frighten me.

Bitzer   I can tell you multiplications tables. Then you'll do better at school.

Sissy   The teachers will teach me, not you.

Bitzer   But I know multiplications. I can tell you them.

Sissy   Leave me alone.

She runs away again, crashing into **Gradgrind** *and* **Bounderby**, *as* **Bitzer** *pulls up.*

Gradgrind   Girl number twenty, Cecilia Jupe, why are you tearing about in this improper manner?

Sissy   I was run after, sir.

Gradgrind   Bitzer! What are you doing running after Jupe?

Bitzer   I wasn't, sir. Not till she run away from me.

Bounderby   Another one chasing after this stroller's girl. You'd have had the whole school peeping at the circus within a week.

Gradgrind   Truly, I think so. Bitzer, turn you about and take yourself home. And don't let me catch you around the horse-riding again.

Bitzer   Yes sir. Definition of a horse. Quadruped. Gramnivorous. Forty teeth, namely twenty-four grinders, four eye-teeth and twelve incisive. Sheds coat in spring. Hoofs hard, but requiring to be shod with iron. Age known by marks in mouth. Sir.

Bitzer *blinks, knuckles his forehead and exits.*

Gradgrind   Jupe, stay here a moment.

Bounderby   What's in the bottle?

Gradgrind   What have you got in that bottle?

Bounderby   Gin.

Sissy   Dear me, no, sir! It's the nine oils.

Bounderby   The what?

Sissy   The nine oils, sir. Father sent me to the town to fetch some. It's what our people always use, sir, when they get any hurts in the ring. They bruise themselves very bad sometimes.

Bounderby Serves 'em right for being idle.

Gradgrind May we speak to your father, Jupe?

Sissy I shall find him directly, sir.

Sissy *exits.*

Bounderby What a place, this, for a self-made man.

Bounderby *jumps, as* **The Wild Huntsman of the Prairies** *suddenly appears. His costume is that of a fantastical Cowboy, but his accent isn't.*

Huntsman By your leave, gentlemen. Did I hear you're come to see Signor Jupe?

Gradgrind Yes.

Enter **Snake Charmer** *(with snake).*

. . . though we can't wait.

Bounderby You see, my friend, we are the kind of people who know the value of time, and you are the kind of people who don't know the value of time.

Huntsman If you mean that you can make more money of your time than I can make of mine, I should judge from your appearance that you are about right.

Charmer And if you want to cheek us, pay at the doors.

Huntsman Sirs, you may or you may not be aware (for perhaps you have not been much in the audience), that Jupe has missed his tip very often lately.

Gradgrind Has – what has he missed?

Charmer His tip. Missed his tip and was loose in his ponging.

Huntsman Didn't do what he ought to do.

Bounderby Nine oils, missing tips, ponging! Queer sort of company too for a man who has raised himself.

Huntsman   He was goosed last night. He was goosed the night before, he was goosed today.

Gradgrind   Why has he been – so very much – goosed?

Huntsman   His joints are turning stiff and he is getting used up.

Charmer   He has his points as a cackler still, but he can't get a living out of them.

Gradgrind   If you please, I will leave a message for Jupe.

Huntsman   Then my opinion is he'll never receive it. It's pretty plain to me, he's off.

Charmer   He's gone.

Gradgrind   Do you mean that he has deserted his daughter?

Charmer   It cut the man deeper that his daughter knew of his being goosed.

Bounderby   Ha! Now, I'll tell you what. I know what these things are. You may be astonished to hear it, but my mother – ran away from me.

Charmer   No, I'm not astonished at all.

Huntsman   Jupe sent his daughter out on an errand not an hour ago, and then was seen to slip out himself, with a bundle tied up. She will never believe it of him, but he has cut away and left her.

Charmer   Poor Sissy! He had better have apprenticed her. Now he leaves her without anything to take to.

Huntsman   Her father always had it in his head that she was to be educated – and when she got into the school here, he was as pleased as Punch. I suppose he had this move in his mind, and considered her provided for . . .

Gradgrind   But I came to tell him that her connections made her not an object for the school, and that she must not attend any more.

Enter **Sleary**.

Sleary   Evening Squire. This is a bad piece of business, this is. You've heard of my clown and his dog being supposed to have morrised?

Gradgrind   Yes.

Sleary   If you should happen to have looked in tonight for the purpose of telling him you were going to do his daughter any little service, it would be fortunate and well-timed . . .

Enter **Sissy** *at a run. She looks around the assembled company . . .*

Sissy   No!

Faced with the incontrovertible truth she dissolves into heartbreak.

Sleary   It's a shame, upon my soul it is.

Sissy   Oh my dear father! You're gone to try to do me some good, I know. But how miserable and helpless you will be without me, poor, poor father.

Huntsman   Those two were one.

Charmer   They were never asunder.

Bounderby   Now, good people all, this is wanton waste of time. Let the girl understand the fact. Let her take it from me, if you like, who have been run away from, myself. Here, what's your name! Your father has absconded – deserted you – and you mustn't expect to see him again as long as you live.

Stony silence. **Gradgrind** *steps up, more gently . . .*

Gradgrind   Jupe – I came here to inform your father that you could not be received at my school any more due to his employment, but am prepared in these altered circumstances to make a proposal. I am willing to take charge of you, Jupe, and to educate you, and provide for you. The only condition I make is that if you decide to accompany me now, it is understood that you communicate no more with any of your friends who are here present.

Sleary   At the same time, I must put in my word. If you like, Cecilia to be 'prenticed, you know the nature of the work and you know your companions. Miss Josephine would be a sister to you, and all our friends here a mother and father to you. There, I've said my say.

Gradgrind   The only observation I will make to you, Jupe, in the way of influencing your decision, is that it is highly desirable to have a sound practical education, and that even your father himself appears to have known and felt that much.

Sissy *stops crying and looks at* **Gradgrind**.

Be sure you know your own mind, Jupe.

Pause.

Sissy   Give me my clothes. Give me my clothes and let me go away before I break my heart.

Snake Charmer *and* **Huntsman** *exit to fetch* **Sissy***'s belongings*.

Bounderby   Gradgrind, I advise against this venture. What of Louisa?

Gradgrind   This may serve as an example to her, of what vulgar curiosity leads to in the end. Think of it, Bounderby, in that point of view.

Bounderby   No. I say no. I say by no means.

Sleary   Goodbye, my dear. You'll make your fortune, I hope. There she is, Squire.

Snake Charmer *returns with* **Sissy***'s belongings in a basket*.

Sleary   Leave the nine oils, Sissy. It's no use to you now. Give it to me.

Sissy   Pray, let me keep it for father, till he comes back. He will want it then.

Sleary   So be it, my dear.

Gradgrind   Now Jupe, if you are quite determined – come.

Sleary   Farewell, Cecilia. Be obedient to the squire and forget us. But if, when you're grown up, you come upon any horse-riding ever – don't be hard upon it. People must be amused, Squire, somehow. They can't be always a working, nor a learning. I lay down the philosophy on the subject when I say to you, Squire, make the best of us, not the worst.

Exit **Sissy**, *with* **Gradgrind** *and* **Bounderby**. *Music –* **Sleary**'s *song.*

All (*Sing.*)   Graceful, gliding! (*Bell, whistle, cymbal!*)

Sleary   Bold and bright, all for your delight.

All   Bareback riding! (*Horn, whiz, cymbal!*)

Run away, run away, run away with us tonight.

The Circus leaves town.

Scene Four

A Coketown Street

A factory hooter.

A solitary female figure enters in the gloom – **Rachael**. *Followed a moment later by a man –* **Stephen Blackpool**.

Stephen   Rachael! (*Catching her up.*) I thought thou wast behind me. Early tonight, lass.

Rachael   'Times I'm a little early, Stephen. 'Times a little late. I'm never to be counted on, going home.

Stephen   Nor going t'other way, neither, 't seems to me, Rachael.

Rachael   No, Stephen. That's how it is. Lift up thy head, lad. (*Looks into his face, questioning.*)

Stephen   Rachael. She's back. I come home last night and there she was, claiming her rights of me and all that's mine.

Rachael   Drunk.

Stephen   Drunk and filthy and . . .

Rachael   And sick?

Stephen   She's been wounded, I think – though I couldn'a get near her. I'm desperate, Rachael. I'm without a hope. I never hurt a livin' creature, but / . . .

Rachael   Say no more. No more, Stephen. I'll come with thee, and sit by her and tend her. I'll do what little I can.

Stephen   If she were to die . . .

Rachael   I know your heart, and am right sure and certain that 'tis far too merciful to let her suffer for want of aid. Thou art not the man to cast the last stone, Stephen, when she is brought so low.

Stephen   Oh Rachael, Rachael.

Rachael   Thou hast been a cruel sufferer, Heaven reward thee. But when she gets better, Stephen, tis to be hoped she'll leave thee to thyself again, and do thee no more hurt.

Stephen   Thou'rt an angel.

Rachael   I'm thy poor friend, Stephen. We are old friends.

Stephen   Thou'rt as young as ever.

Rachael   Come lad. I'll go with thee now.

Stephen   It might make folk talk . . .

Rachael   When they hear she's back again, they'll know why I'm there. And after that, as always, tis better that we don't walk too much together.

Stephen   Thou hast been that good to me, Rachael, through so many years, that thy word is a law to me. Ay, lass, and a bright good law. Better than some real ones.

Rachael   Oh, Stephen. Let the laws be.

Stephen   Ay. Let 'em be.

Scene Five

The Gradgrinds' Parlour

Louisa *and* **Sissy**, *doing mathematics together.* **Sissy** *almost in tears.*

Sissy   'Name the cost of two hundred and forty-seven muslin caps at fourteen-pence halfpenny.'

Louisa   Stay calm, Sissy, and think of it logically. It sounds complicated, but in fact it's simply two numbers that must be multiplied together. I'll write the sum out for you . . .

Louisa *begins to write on a slate, as* **Sissy** *looks on in admiration.*

Sissy   It would be a fine thing to be you, Miss Louisa.

Louisa   Do you think so?

Sissy   I should know so much, Miss Louisa. All that is difficult to me now, would be so easy then.

Louisa   You might not be the better for it, Sissy.

Sissy   I should not be the worse.

Louisa   I don't know that. You are more useful to my mother, and more pleasant with her than I can ever be.

Sissy   But, if you please, Miss Louisa, I am – oh so stupid.

Louisa   You will be wiser by and by.

Sissy   You don't know what a stupid girl I am. All through school hours I make mistakes. I can't help them.

Louisa   We all make mistakes, Sissy.

Sissy   Today, for instance, the teacher was explaining to us about Natural Prosperity.

Louisa   National, I think it must have been.

Sissy   Yes, it was. National Prosperity. And he said, 'now this school room is a nation. And in the nation there are fifty millions of money. Isn't this a prosperous nation? Girl number twenty, isn't this a prosperous nation, and a'n't you living in a thriving state?'

Louisa   What did you say?

Sissy   Miss Louisa, I said I couldn't know whether it was a prosperous nation or not unless I knew who had got the money, and whether any of it was mine. But that had nothing to do with it. I shall never learn. And the worst of all is, that although my poor father wished me so much to learn, and although I am very anxious to learn, I am afraid I don't like it.

Louisa   Did your father know so much himself, that he wished you to be well taught too, Sissy?

Sissy   No, Miss Louisa. Father knows very little indeed. It's as much as he can do to write.

Louisa   Your mother?

Sissy   She died when I was born. She was . . . she was a dancer!

Louisa   Did your father love her?

Sissy   Oh yes. Father loved me, first, for her sake. He carried me about with him when I was quite a baby. We have never been asunder from that time.

Louisa   Yet he leaves you now, Sissy.

Sissy   He will not be happy for a single minute till he comes back.

Louisa   Tell me more about him.

Sissy   We travelled about the country, and had no fixed place to live in.

Father's a . . . a clown.

Louisa   To make the people laugh?

Sissy   Yes, but they wouldn't laugh sometimes, and then father cried. Lately they very often wouldn't laugh, and he'd come home despairing. I used to read to him to cheer his courage. They were wrong books – I am never to speak of them here – but we didn't know there was any harm in them.

Louisa   And he liked them?

Sissy   Oh, very much. Often of a night he used to forget all his troubles in wondering whether the Sultan would let the lady go on with the story, or would have her head cut off before it was finished.

Louisa   And your father was always kind?

Sissy   Always, always. Kinder than I can tell. He was unkind only one night, and that was not to me, but Merrylegs, his . . . performing dog.

Louisa   Was he angry with the dog?

Sissy   Everything of Father's had gone wrong that night, and he hadn't pleased the public at all. He cried out that the very dog knew he was failing, and had no compassion on him. Then he beat the dog, and I was frightened, and said, 'Father, Father! O Heaven forgive you, Father, stop.' And he stopped, and the dog was bloody and Father lay down crying on the floor with the dog in his arms and the dog licked his face.

Sissy *is crying now.*

Louisa *takes* **Sissy**'s *hand and kisses her.*

He hasn't left me for good, Miss Louisa. I know he'll come back for me.

Louisa   Is that why you always ask if there's a letter for you?

Sissy   I know it vexes your father and mother so, but I must hope.

Louisa   Hope. Can hope take hold of the mind as much as a fact?

Sissy   I keep the bottle of nine oils always. Ready for when he returns.

Scene Six

Bounderby's Parlour

Mr Bounderby, *at lunch*, **Mrs Sparsit** *enters*.

Sparsit   Mr Bounderby, you are unusually slow with your lunch today.

Bounderby   Why, ma'am, I am thinking about Thomas Gradgrind's whim of bringing up the tumbling girl. It's tolerably clear to me that Louisa can get small good out of such companionship.

Sparsit   You are quite another father to Louisa, sir.

Bounderby   If you had said I was another father to young Tom, you might have been nearer the mark. I am going to take young Tom into my office. Going to have him under my wing, Mrs Sparsit.

Sparsit   He is a very fortunate young man.

Bounderby   Egad, ma'am, so he is. And he'd open his eyes that boy would, if he knew my experience at his time of life – with only a bed on the pavement. People like you, Mrs Sparsit ma'am, accustomed from infancy to lie on down feathers, have no idea how hard a paving stone is without trying it.

Sparsit   Indeed.

Bounderby   As I have raised myself up, you have fallen, Mrs Sparsit.

Sparsit   I have.

Bounderby   You were in born into crack society.

Sparsit   It is true sir.

Bounderby   Devilish high society.

Sparsit   Sir, I'm here to inform you that once you have finished your lunch, there is one of the hands from the mill wishes to speak with you.

Bounderby   What's the name of this Hand?

Sparsit   One Stephen Blackpool.

Bounderby   Let him come in now.

Sparsit   Yes sir.

Bounderby   There is nothing troublesome in Stephen Blackpool.

Sparsit (*At the door.*)   You may come in.

Enter **Stephen**.

Bounderby   Now Stephen, what's the matter? We never have any difficulty with you. You have never been one of the unreasonable ones. You don't expect to be set up in a coach and six, and to be fed on turtle soup and venison, with a gold spoon, as a good many of 'em do. Therefore I know you have not come here to make a complaint.

Stephen   No, sir, sure I haven't come for nowt o' the kind.

Bounderby   Then let me hear what it is. Out with it lad.

Stephen *hesitates, glancing at* **Mrs Sparsit**.

Sparsit   I can go, Mr Bounderby, if you wish it.

Bounderby   This good lady, Mrs Sparsit, is a born lady. You are not to suppose because she keeps my house for me that she hasn't been very high up the tree – up at the top of the tree. Now if you have got anything to say that can't be said before a born lady, this lady will leave the room. If what you have got to say can be said before a born lady, this lady will stay where she is.

Stephen   Sir, I hope I never had nowt to say not fit for a born lady to hear, sin I was born myseln.

Bounderby   Very well. Fire away.

Stephen   I've come to ask your advice. I were married on Easter Monday nineteen year since. She were a young lass, pretty enough, wi' a good account of herseln. Well. She went bad – soon. Not along of me. God knows, I were not an unkind husband to her.

Bounderby   I have heard all this before. She took to drinking, left off working, sold the furniture, pawned the clothes / . . .

Stephen   I tried to wean her from it – not once – but twenty time. She left me.

She disgraced herseln everyways, and then she come back. She come back, she come back. I walked the streets nights long, ere ever I'd go home. I ha gone t' th' brigg, minded to fling myseln ower and ha' no more on't. These five year I ha' paid her to keep away from me. I ha' gotten decent furniture about me again. I lived, not fearful for the minutes of my life. Two nights ago I went home and there she lay upon the hearth stone. There she is.

Bounderby   It's a bad job, that's what it is. You had better have been satisfied as you were and not have got married. However it's too late to say that.

Sparsit   Was it an unequal marriage, sir, in point of years?

Stephen   Not e'en so. I were one and twenty myseln, and she were twenty.

Sparsit   Indeed, sir? I inferred, from its being so miserable a marriage that it was probably an unequal one in point of years.

Bounderby *eyeballs* **Sparsit** *and helps himself to a sherry.*

Stephen   I've come to ask you, sir, how I am to be ridded o' this woman.

Bounderby   What do you mean?

Stephen   I cannot bear it no more. I ha lived under it so long, and but for the pity and comforting words of the best lass living or dead, I'd have gone battering mad.

Sparsit   I fear, sir, he wishes to be free to marry the female of whom he speaks.

Stephen   I do. I've heard that great folk are not bonded together for better for worst so fast, but that they can be set free from their misfortunate marriages and marry again. They can be set free for smaller wrongs than mine. I mun be ridden of this woman, and I want to know how.

Bounderby   How?

Stephen   If I do her any hurt there's a law to punish me.

Bounderby   Of course there is.

Stephen   If I flee from her there's a law to punish me.

Sparsit   Of course there is.

Stephen   If I was to live wi' t'other dear lass, an' not marry her – which it never could be, and her so good – there's a law to punish me and every innocent child belonging to me.

Both   Of course there is!

Stephen   Now a' God's name, show me the law to help me.

Bounderby   There's a sanctity in this relationship of life, and it must be kept up.

Stephen   Dunnot say that, sir. I read in the papers how the impossibility of ever getting unchained from one another brings many common married folk to battle and murder. Mine's a grievous case, an' I want – if you will be so good – to know the law that helps me.

Bounderby   Now, I'll tell you what, there is such a law. But it's not for you at all. It costs money – a mint of money.

Stephen   How much?

Bounderby   You'd have to go to Doctors' Commons, a court of Common Law, and the House of Lords with a suit, and then you'd have to get an Act of Parliament to enable you to marry again / . . .

Stephen   How much?

Bounderby   I suppose, from a thousand to fifteen hundred pound. Perhaps twice that.

Stephen   There's no other law?

Bounderby   Certainly not.

Stephen   Why then, tis a muddle. And the sooner I am dead, the better.

Bounderby   Pooh, pooh! Don't talk nonsense, my good fellow, about things you don't understand. And don't you call the institutions of your country a muddle. With what I call your unhallowed opinions, you have been quite shocking this lady, who, as I have already told, is a born lady, and who, as I have not already told you, has had her own marriage misfortunes! The institutions of your country are not your piece-work.

You didn't take your wife for fast and for loose; but for better for worse. If she has turned out worse – why, all we have got to say is, she might have turned out better.

Scene Seven

A Coketown Street

Mrs Pegler – *a dignified old lady, in travelling clothes – gazing up at the house of* **Mr Bounderby**.

Enter **Stephen Blackpool**.

Mrs Pegler   Pray sir, didn't I see you come out of that gentleman's house?

Stephen   Yes, missus, it were me.

Mrs Pegler   Have you – you'll excuse an old woman's curiosity – have you seen the gentleman?

Stephen   Yes, missus.

Mrs Pegler   And how did he look, sir? Was he portly, bold, outspoken and hearty?

Stephen   Oh yes. He were all that.

Mrs Pegler   And healthy, as the fresh wind?

Stephen   Yes, he were eatin' and drinkin' as large and as loud as a hummobee.

Mrs Pegler   Thank you. Thank you.

Stephen   Good day to you, missus. I mun be getting back to work.

Mrs Pegler   You work for the gentleman?

Stephen   That I do. In his mill.

Mrs Pegler   You must be very happy.

Stephen   !

Mrs Pegler   How long have you worked for the gentleman?

Stephen   A dozen year or more.

Mrs Pegler   I must kiss the hand that has worked for this fine gentleman for a dozen year.

Stephen   Do you come from the country, missus?

Mrs Pegler   Yes. I came forty mile by Parliamentary this morning, and I'm going back the same forty mile this afternoon. I walked nine mile to the station this morning, and I shall walk the nine mile back tonight. That's pretty well, sir, at my age. Now and then I spend my savings so – to see the gentleman.

Stephen   Only to see him?

Mrs Pegler   That's enough for me. I have been standing about on this side of the way to see that gentleman come out. But he's late this year, and now, I'm obliged to go without a glimpse of him. But I have seen you, and you have seen him, and I must make that do.

Stephen   It should be enough for you, I'm sure, missus. T'would be more than enough for me.

Mrs Pegler   He is a great man of business.

Stephen   Ay. He has a bank also.

Mrs Pegler   Bounderby's Bank!

Stephen   Ay. He knows how to do arithmetic, missus. Better than most.

Scene Eight

The Gradgrinds' Parlour

Tom *and* **Louisa**.

Tom   I am sick of my life, Loo. I hate it altogether, and I hate everybody except you.

Louisa   You don't hate Sissy, Tom.

Tom   I hate to be obliged to call her Jupe. And she hates me. I don't blame her. Father was determined to make me a donkey and that's what I am. I am as obstinate as one, and I should like to kick like one.

Louisa   Not me, I hope, Tom.

Tom   No, Loo. I wouldn't hurt you. I don't know what this jolly old jaundiced jail would be without you.

Louisa   But I don't know what other girls know. I can't play to you, or sing to you to lighten your mind when you're tired.

Tom   I wish I could collect all the Facts we hear so much about, and all the Figures, and all the people who found them out; and put a thousand barrels of gunpowder under them and blow them all up. But when I go to live with old Bounderby, I'll have my revenge. I'll enjoy myself a little.

Louisa   Do you look forward to the change to Mr Bounderby's?

Tom   Why, there's one thing to be said of it, it will be getting away from home. And I'll go about and see something and hear something. I'll recompense myself for the way in which I have been brought up.

Louisa   But Mr Bounderby thinks as father thinks, and is not half so kind.

Tom   Oh. I know how to manage and smooth old Bounderby.

Louisa   You do? How? Is it a secret?

Tom   If it's a secret, it's not far off. It's you. You are his little pet. He'll do anything for you. When he says to me what I don't like, I shall say to him, 'My sister Loo will be hurt and disappointed, Mr Bounderby. She always used to tell me she was sure you would be easier with me than this'. That'll bring him about, or nothing will.

Pause.

Have you gone to sleep, Loo?

Louisa   No, Tom. I'm looking at the fire.

Tom   You seem to find more to look at in it than ever I could find. Except that it's a fire, it looks to me as stupid and blank as everything else looks.

What do you see in it? Not a circus?

Music – far off . . .

Mr Sleary *and other figures of the circus enter in the shadows – humming the tune to* **Sleary***'s opening song.*

Louisa   I have been wondering about you and me, grown up.

Tom   Wondering!

Louisa   I have such unmanageable thoughts, that they will wonder.

Sleary   Hurry ladies. Hurry gentlemen – to see Tom and Louisa Gradgrind, grown up!

Cupid takes **Louisa**'*s child's pinny and hands her the shawl and indoor bonnet of a young woman.*

Get your ticket for a ringside seat to see Tom Gradgrind move to Mr Bounderby's house and begin work at the Bank.

Strong Man *brings* **Tom** *a top hat and tail coat.*

Gasp, as Mr Gradgrind is elected Member of Parliament for Coketown.

Mr Gradgrind *enters, and the* **Snake Charmer** *pins on him a political rosette.*

Rock with laughter as the young clown Mamselle Jupe carries on a-tumbling in the Gradgrind household.

Sissy *enters, dressed more maturely now.*

Hurry, hurry, it's all here – the slack wire, the tight rope, knife-throwers, jugglers, acrobatics, snake-charmers and fire-eaters . . .

All (*Sing in a whisper.*)   Run away, run away, run away with us tonight.

The sounds of the Circus now echo far off, as **Louisa** *is once more back at her place by the fire – lost in her reverie.*

Scene Nine

Gradgrind's study

Sissy *and* **Gradgrind**.

Gradgrind   I fear, Jupe, that your continuance at the school any longer would be useless.

Sissy   I am afraid it would, sir.

Gradgrind   I cannot disguise from you, Jupe, that the result of your probation there has greatly disappointed me. You have not acquired anything like that amount of exact knowledge which I looked for. You are altogether backward, and below the mark.

Sissy   I am sorry, sir. Yet I have tried.

Gradgrind   Yes, I believe you have; I can find no fault in that respect. I can only suppose that the circumstances of your early life were unfavourable to the development of your reasoning powers, and that we began too late.

Sissy   I wish I could have made a better acknowledgement, sir, of your kindness to a poor forlorn girl . . .

Gradgrind   Don't shed tears. I don't complain of you.

Sissy   Thank you, sir, very much.

Gradgrind   You are useful to Mrs Gradgrind; so I understand from Miss Louisa, and, indeed so I have observed myself. My new duties as Member of Parliament for Coketown will take me away from home a good deal, and your remaining within this household as companion and friend to the family is a most serviceable fact, therefore I hope that you can make yourself happy in those relations.

Sissy   I should have nothing to wish, sir, if only / . . .

Gradgrind   I understand; you refer to your father. I have heard from Miss Louisa that you still preserve that bottle of nine oils. Well. If your training in the science of arriving at exact results had been more successful, you would have been wiser on these points.

Sissy   Yes sir. Thank you, sir.

Gradgrind   You are an affectionate, earnest, good young woman – and – we must make that do.

Scene Ten

The Gradgrinds' Parlour

Louisa *gazing at the fire. Enter* **Tom**.

Tom Are you there, Loo?

Louisa Tom! Dear Tom, how long it is since you've been to see me.

Tom I have been otherwise engaged, Loo, in the evenings; and in the daytime old Bounderby has been keeping me at it rather. I say, has Father said anything particular to you today or yesterday, Loo?

Louisa No, Tom.

Tom Do you know where he is tonight?

Louisa No.

Tom Then I'll tell you, he's with old Bounderby. They are having a regular confab together up at the Bank.

Louisa At the Bank?

Tom To keep Mrs Sparsit's ears as far off as possible, I expect. You are very fond of me, an't you, Loo?

Louisa Indeed I am, Tom, though you do let such long intervals go by without coming to see me.

Tom We might be so much oftener together – mightn't we? Always together, almost – mightn't we? It would do me a great deal of good if you were to make up your mind to I know what, Loo. It would be a splendid thing for me. It would be uncommonly jolly.

Enter **Gradgrind**.

Father!

Gradgrind Good evening, Tom. I wasn't expecting you tonight.

Tom   I can't stay. I'm engaged to some fellows tonight. Goodbye Louisa. (*He embraces* **Louisa** *and whispers.*) You won't forget how fond you are of me?

Louisa   No, Tom, I won't forget.

Tom   That's a capital girl. Good evening, Father.

Gradgrind   Tom.

Exit **Tom**. *Long pause.*

Gradgrind   My dear Louisa, you are a woman.

Louisa   Yes, Father.

Gradgrind   I must speak with you, and seriously.

Louisa   Yes, Father?

Gradgrind   You have been well trained, and I have perfect confidence in your good sense. You are not impulsive, you are not romantic, and I know you will consider what I am going to communicate from the ground of reason and calculation. Louisa, my dear, you are the subject of a proposal of marriage that has been made to me.

Louisa *is impassive.*

A proposal of marriage, my dear.

Louisa   I hear you, Father. I am attending, I assure you.

Gradgrind   Well, you are even more dispassionate than I expected, Louisa. Or perhaps you are not unprepared for the announcement I have it in charge to make.

Louisa   I cannot say that, Father, until I hear it. Prepared or unprepared, I wish to hear you state it to me.

Gradgrind   I have undertaken then to let you know that – in short – that Mr Bounderby has informed me that he has watched you progress with particular interest, and has long hoped that the time might ultimately arrive when he should offer you his hand in marriage. He has made his proposal of marriage to me, and has entreated me to make it known to you, and to express his hope that you will take it into your favourable consideration.

Long pause.

Louisa   Father, do you think I love Mr Bounderby?

Gradgrind   Well my child. I – really – cannot take upon myself to say.

Louisa   Father, do you ask me to love Mr Bounderby?

Gradgrind   My dear Louisa, no. No. I ask nothing.

Louisa   Father, does Mr Bounderby ask me to love him?

Gradgrind   Mr Bounderby does not do you the injustice of pretending to anything fanciful or sentimental. Therefore, perhaps the expression itself – I merely suggest this to you, my dear – may be a little misplaced.

Louisa   What would you advise me to use in its stead, Father?

Gradgrind   There is some disparity in age. Yet I find, in reference to the statistics obtained in England and Wales, that a large proportion of marriages are contracted between parties of very unequal ages, and that the elder of these contracting parties is, in rather more than three-quarters of these instances, the bridegroom.

Louisa   What do you recommend, Father, that I should substitute for the expression I used just now, for the misplaced term – love?

Gradgrind   Louisa, confine yourself rigidly to Fact. The question of Fact you state to yourself is: does Mr Bounderby ask me to marry him? Yes, he does. The sole remaining question then is: shall I marry him? I think nothing can be plainer than that.

Louisa   Shall I marry him.

Gradgrind   Precisely. Now, I have stated the case, as such cases are usually stated among practical minds. The rest, my dear Louisa, is for you to decide.

Louisa *moves away and contemplates something in the far distance – as if through a window.*

Are you consulting the chimneys of Coketown, Louisa?

Louisa   There seems to be nothing there but languid and monotonous smoke. Yet when the night comes, fire bursts out.

Gradgrind   I do not see the application of that remark.

Louisa   I have often thought that life is very short.

Gradgrind   It is. Still, the average duration of human life is proved to have increased in recent years.

Louisa   I speak of my own life, Father. While it lasts, I would wish to do the little I can, and the little I am fit for. What does it matter?

Gradgrind   What matter, my dear?

Louisa   Mr Bounderby asks me to marry him. The question I have to ask myself is, shall I marry him?

Gradgrind   That is so.

Louisa   Then, since Mr Bounderby likes to take me thus, I am satisfied to accept his proposal. Tell him, Father, that this was my answer. Repeat it, word for word, because I should wish him to know what I said.

Gradgrind   It is quite right my dear, to be exact. I will observe your very proper request. (*A sudden thought strikes him.*) Louisa, perhaps I ought to ask you – you have never entertained in secret any other proposal?

Louisa   Father, what other proposal can have been made to me? Whom have I seen? Where have I been? What are my heart's experiences?

Gradgrind   My dear Louisa, you correct me justly.

Louisa   What do I know of tastes and fancies; of aspirations and affections?

Gradgrind   My dear, quite true, quite true.

Louisa   What a strange question to ask me. You have dealt so wisely with me, Father, from my cradle to this hour, that I never had a child's belief or a child's fear. I never had a child's heart. Never dreamed a child's dream.

Gradgrind   My dear Louisa, you abundantly repay my care. I may assure you now, my child, that I am made happy by the sound decision at which you have arrived. Mr Bounderby is a very remarkable man. Kiss me, my dear girl.

Enter **Mrs Gradgrind**, *with* **Sissy** *following*.

Mrs G   Have you settled it then? Well, Louisa, I hope your health may be good; for if your head begins to split as soon as you are married, which was the case with mine, I cannot consider that you are to be envied. I must give you a kiss of congratulation, but don't touch my right shoulder, for there's something running down it all day long.

Sissy   What's settled?

Gradgrind   Good news, Jupe. Louisa has accepted a proposal of marriage!

Sissy   Who from?

Gradgrind   From whom, Jupe. From whom.

Sissy   From whom?

Gradgrind   Mr Bounderby!

Mrs G   Oh, but what am I to call him?

Sissy   Is it true, Miss Louisa?

Mrs G   I must call him something. I cannot call him Josiah, but am I to call my own son-in-law Mister?

Sissy   Mr Bounderby?

Mrs G   As to the wedding, all I ask, Louisa, is that it may take place soon. Otherwise I know it is one of those subjects I shall never hear the last of.

Gradgrind   Jupe, aren't you going to congratulate Miss Louisa?

Sissy   Yes. Congratulations.

Mrs G   Come, Mr Gradgrind, my head is splitting, yet I must consult you on what I am to call Mr Bounderby once they are married – or I shall be worrying myself morning, noon and night.

Gradgrind   Yes, my dear, but first, I shall impart to Mr Bounderby the news of his happiness.

Exit **Mr** *and* **Mrs Gradgrind**. **Sissy** *gazes at* **Louisa**.

Sissy   Mr Bounderby? Oh Louisa / . . .

Louisa   *Miss* Louisa. And when I am married I shall be Mrs Bounderby. And I will go to live in the town with Tom.

Sissy   But / . . .

Louisa   You no doubt will remain here, until you marry – if you ever do.

Sissy   Yes.

Louisa   And now perhaps you should attend on my mother. She has a headache I think.

Sissy   Yes, Miss Louisa.

Sissy *exits and* **Louisa** *turns an inscrutable face back to the fire.*

Scene Eleven

Bounderby's Parlour

Mrs Sparsit *seated – picking at some cambric with a pair of very sharp scissors. Enter* **Bounderby**.

Sparsit   Good evening, Mr Bounderby.

Bounderby   Good evening, ma'am, good evening.

Sparsit   You are unusually late this evening, Mr Bounderby.

Bounderby   Indeed ma'am. I had occasion to speak with Tom Gradgrind.

Sparsit   On a matter concerning the school?

Bounderby   No, not the school.

Sparsit   The Bank, perhaps?

Bounderby   Not the Bank.

Sparsit   Then the mill? Is there a difficulty at the mill? But then, why should that concern Mr Thomas Gradgrind?

Bounderby   It is no concern of anyone's.

Sparsit   Nor mine, I'm sure.

Bounderby   Mrs Sparsit, ma'am, you are not only a lady born and bred, but a devilish sensible woman.

Sparsit   Sir, this is indeed not the first time that you have honoured me with similar expressions of your good opinion.

Bounderby   Mrs Sparsit, ma'am, I am going to astonish you.

Sparsit   Yes, sir?

Bounderby   I am going to, ma'am – to marry Tom Gradgrind's daughter.

Sparsit   Yes, sir. I hope you may be happy, Mr Bounderby. Oh, indeed, I hope you may be happy, sir.

Bounderby   You do?

Sparsit   I wish with all my heart, sir, that you may be in all respects very happy.

Bounderby   Well, ma'am. I am obliged to you. I hope I shall be.

Sparsit   Do you, sir? But naturally you do; of course you do.

Pause.

Bounderby   Well, ma'am, under these circumstances, I imagine it would not be agreeable to a character like yours to remain here, though you would be very welcome here.

Sparsit   Oh, dear no, sir. I could on no account think of that.

Bounderby   However, ma'am, there are apartments at the Bank, where a born-and-bred lady, as keeper of the place, would be rather a catch than otherwise, and if the same pay / . . .

Sparsit   I beg your pardon, sir. You were so good as to promise that you would always substitute the phrase, 'annual compliment'.

Bounderby   If the same 'annual compliment' would be acceptable there, why, I see nothing to part us, unless you do?

Sparsit   Sir, if the position I shall assume at the Bank is one that I could occupy without descending lower in the social scale / . . .

Bounderby   Why of course it is. If it was not, ma'am, you don't suppose that I should offer it to a lady who has moved in the society you have moved in?

Sparsit   Mr Bounderby, you are very considerate.

Bounderby   You'll have your own private apartments, and you'll have your coals and your candles and all the rest of it; a maid, and you'll have the light porter, young Bitzer, to protect you.

Sparsit   Sir, say no more. I shall not be freed from the necessity of eating the bread of dependence, but I would rather receive it from your hand, than from any other.

Therefore, sir, I accept your offer gratefully. And I hope, sir, I fondly hope that Miss Gradgrind may be all you desire, and deserve.

Scene Twelve

The Wedding

Music – solemn and spare, played on a single instrument. **Louisa** *is there suddenly, a modest, impassive bride.*

Mr Gradgrind *enters to lead his daughter to her new husband.* **Mrs Gradgrind**, *dabbing her eyes.*

The lovers meet.

Tom *and* **Sissy** *join.* **Tom**, *drunk.* **Sissy**, *subdued. A toast!*

Musical pause . . .

Bounderby   Ladies and Gentlemen, I am Josiah Bounderby of Coketown. Since you have done my wife and myself the honour of drinking our healths and happiness, I suppose I must acknowledge the same; though, as you all know me, and know what I am, and what my extraction was, you won't expect a speech. If you want a speech this morning, my friend and father-in-law Tom Gradgrind is a Member of Parliament, and you know where to get it.

I am this day married to Tom Gradgrind's daughter. I am very glad to be so. I have watched her bringing-up and I believe she is worthy of me. At the same time, I believe I am worthy of her. So, I thank you, on both our parts, and I hope every bachelor may find as good a wife as I have found. And I hope every spinster may find as good a husband as my wife has found.

Applause.

I give you a toast, ladies and gentlemen – to Mrs Bounderby, the bride.

All   The Bride. *Applause and hand shaking etc . . .* **Tom** *comes up behind* **Louisa**.

Tom   I say, Loo – what a game girl you are to be such a first-rate sister.

Louisa   I'll be nearer to you again now I'll be living at Mr Bounderby's, too. We can be together so much more often.

Tom   Yes. It's done me a great deal of good you taking old Bounderby. It's a splendid thing.

Louisa   Oh Tom.

She clings to him.

Tom   Time's up, Loo. I'm meeting some fellows tonight, and old Bounderby's quite ready for your honeymoon. I shall be on the look-out for you when you get back. Goodbye.

Tom *prises himself from the arms of the trembling* **Louisa**, *and passes her to* **Bounderby**.

Music picks up . . .

As **Louisa** *and* **Bounderby** *exit,* **Tom** *calls after them.*

I say, my dear Loo. Aint it uncommonly jolly now!

Interlude – The weavers gather for their meeting

Music – traditional tune: The Four Loom Weaver. (The tone is proud and defiant.)

All (*Sing.*)
   I'm a four loom weaver as many a one knows
   I've nowt to eat and I've worn out me clothes
   Me clogs are both broken, and stockings I've none
   Tha'd scarce give me tuppence for a' I've gotten on.

   Owd Billy o't Bent he kept telling me long
   We might have better times if I'd nobbut howd me tongue
   Well I've howden me tongue till I near lost me breath
   And I feel in my heart that I'll soon clem to death.

I'm a four loom weaver as many a one knows
I've nowt to eat and I've worn out me clothes
Me clogs are both broken, and stockings I've none
Tha'd scarce give me tuppence for a' I've gotten on.

Scene Thirteen

The room above the Bank

Sparsit *looking from her 'window' as* **Bitzer** *brings in a tray of tea and muffins.*

Sparsit   What are the restless wretches doing now?

Bitzer   Merely going on in the old way, ma'am. Uniting, and leaguing and engaging to stand by one another.

Sparsit   It is much to be regretted that the masters allow of any such class-combinations.

Bitzer   Yes ma'am.

Bitzer *pours tea.*

Sparsit   I do not pretend to understand these things, my lot having been signally cast in a widely different sphere. I only know that these people must be conquered, and that it's high time it was done, once and for all.

Bitzer   Muffin, ma'am?

Sparsit   Thank you, Bitzer.

Bitzer *hands over a cup of tea.*

Sparsit   Has it been a busy day in the Bank, Bitzer?

Bitzer   An average day, ma'am.

Sparsit   The clerks are trustworthy, punctual and industrious of course?

Bitzer   Yes ma'am, pretty fair, ma'am. With the usual exception.

Sparsit Ah. (*Slurps tea.*)

Bitzer Young Mr Thomas Gradgrind, ma'am.

Sparsit Bitzer, do you recollect what I have said to you respecting names?

Bitzer I beg your pardon, ma'am. You did object to names being used.

Sparsit Please to remember, Bitzer, I hold a trust here at the Bank, under Mr Bounderby – and I cannot allow names to be mentioned under this roof that are unfortunately – most unfortunately – connected with his. Mr Bounderby is married to Mr Thomas' sister and therefore, Bitzer, when referring to Mr Thomas, say 'an individual' and I will understand.

Bitzer Yes ma'am. The Bank clerks are all trustworthy, punctual and industrious, with the usual exception of – an individual.

Sparsit Ah. (*Slurp.*)

Bitzer An individual, ma'am, has never been what he ought to have been, since he first came in to the Bank last year. He is a dissipated, extravagant idler.

Sparsit Ah. (*Slurp.*)

Bitzer He is as improvident as any of the people in this town.

Sparsit And we know what their improvidence is.

Bitzer Yes, ma'am. (*Returning to the window.*) This combining together at the Mill will do them no good. I have no doubt that by watching and informing upon one another they could earn a trifle now and then and improve their livelihoods. Then why don't they improve it, ma'am? It's the first consideration of a rational creature. I learnt that at school.

Sparsit They would do well to take example by you, Bitzer.

Bitzer   Yes ma'am. I don't even go to the length of my wages. That's where it is. I have only one to feed, and that's the person I most like to feed.

Sparsit   To be sure.

Bitzer   Would you wish a little more hot water, ma'am, or is there anything else that I could fetch you?

Sparsit   Nothing just now, Bitzer.

Bitzer   Thank you, ma'am. I shouldn't wish to disturb you at your meals, ma'am, particularly tea, knowing your partiality for it; but there's a gentleman down in the street been looking up here for a minute or so, ma'am, and he has come across as if he was going to knock.

Knock knock.

That is his knock, ma'am, no doubt.

Sparsit   What a stranger can want at the Bank at this time of the evening I don't know. But I hold a charge in this establishment for Mr Bounderby, and I will never shrink from it. If to see him is any part of the duty I have accepted, I will see him. Use your own discretion, Bitzer.

Exit **Bitzer**.

Sparsit *prepares herself.*

Scene Fourteen

The Union Meeting

A meeting convenes, and **Mr Slackbridge** *takes up his position as orator.*

Slackbridge   Oh, my friends, the downtrodden operatives of Coketown; slaves of an iron-handed despotism; fellow workmen; fellow men. I tell you that the hour is come, when we must rally round one another as One united power, and crumble into dust the oppressors that too long have battened upon the labour of our hands.

Crowd   Hear, hear, hear! Hurrah! Good!

Slackbridge   Oh, men of Coketown! But what shall we say of that working man who, being well acquainted with the grievances and wrongs of you, resolves not to subscribe to the funds of the United Aggregate Tribunal; who turns a traitor and who is not ashamed to make to you the dastardly avowal that he will hold himself aloof and will not be associated in the gallant stand for Freedom and for Right?

Crowd   Be sure you're right, Slackbridge. Put him up. Let's hear him. Is the man here, Slackbridge? Let's hear the man himself, instead o' you!

Slackbridge   Friends and fellow men. I do not wonder that you are incredulous of the existence of such a man. But Judas Iscariot existed, and this man exists.

Chairman   Friends, by virtue o' my office here as your president, I ask our friend Slackbridge, who may be a little overheated in the business, to take his seat, whiles this man is heard. You all know Stephen Blackpool. You know of his misfortunes and his good name.

Stephen *steps forth from the crowd.*

Stephen   My friends. I have heard what's been spok'n o' me, and 'tis likely that I shan't mend it. But I prefer you heard the truth concernin' myself, from my lips than from onny other man's. I'm th' one single Hand in Bounderby's mill as don't come in wi' the Union. I ha' my reasons – mine, you see – for being hindered; not on'y now, but awlus – awlus – lifelong.

Slackbridge   What but this did I tell you? Oh, my friends, what / . . .

Crowd   Hold thy tongue, Slackbridge. Let the man be heard.

Stephen   My brothers, and my fellow workmen – for that you are to me – I know well, all what's afore me. I know well that you all resolve to have no more ado wi' a man who is not wi' you in the matter.

Chairman   Stephen Blackpool, think on it once again, lad, afore thou'rt shunned by all owd friends.

Stephen   Many's the face I see here, as I first seen when I were young and lighter heart'n than now. I have never had no fratch afore, sin ever I were born, wi' any o' my like; God knows I have none now that's o' my makin'. Truly I must do't, my friends, not to brave you, but to live. I mak no complaints o' being turned to the wall, o' bein outcast and overlooked from this time forrard, but hope I shall be let to work. If there is any right for me at all, my friends I think tis that. Now I tak my leave of all here.

As **Stephen** *exits everyone turns their back to him.*

Slackbridge   The Roman Brutus condemned his own son to death; the Spartan mothers drove their flying children on the points of their enemies' swords – and so we shun this traitor Stephen Blackpool and say three cheers for the United Aggregate Tribunal.

Silence.

Scene Fifteen

The room above the Bank

Mrs Sparsit *has been interviewing* **Mr James Harthouse** *for a short while. He gazes languidly out of the window.*

Harthouse   Exceedingly odd place this, Mrs Sparsit. Will you allow me to ask you, is it always as black as this?

Sparsit   In general, Mr Harthouse, it is much blacker.

Harthouse   Is it possible?

Sparsit   Can I inquire as to the nature of your visit here?

Harthouse   Excuse me, you are not a native, I think.

Sparsit   No sir, it was once my good or ill fortune, as it may be – before I became a widow – to move in a very different sphere.

Harthouse   You must be very bored here.

Sparsit   I am the servant of circumstances, sir, and have long adapted myself to the governing power of my life.

Harthouse   Very philosophical.

Sparsit   May I be permitted to ask, sir, to what I am indebted for the favour of your call?

Harthouse   Assuredly. Much obliged to you for reminding me. Walking through this extraordinarily black town, while they were getting dinner ready at the hotel, I asked a fellow; one of the working people; who appeared to have been taking a shower-bath of something fluffy, which I assume to be the raw material . . .?

Sparsit   Indeed.

Harthouse   I asked where Mr Bounderby might reside. Upon which, he directed me to the Bank. Fact being, I presume that Mr Bounderby the banker does not reside here.

Sparsit   No, sir. He does not.

Harthouse   Thank you. I had no intention of delivering my letter of introduction to Mr Bounderby at the present moment, but strolling on to the Bank to kill time, I had the good fortune to observe at the window, a lady of a very superior and agreeable appearance. I considered that I could not do better than take the liberty of asking that lady where Mr Bounderby the banker does live. Which I accordingly venture, with all suitable apologies, to do.

Sparsit   A letter, sir?

Harthouse   From the Member of Parliament for this place, a Mr Gradgrind – whom I had the pleasure of knowing in London.

Sparsit   Ah yes. I can, of course, furnish you with the address and directions to the home of Mr Bounderby. I will write it down for you.

Harthouse   Thousand thanks. You know him well?

Sparsit   In my dependent relation towards him, I have known him ten years.

Harthouse   I think he is married to Gradgrind's daughter.

Sparsit   Yes. He has that – honour. They have been married just above a year now.

Harthouse   The lady is quite a philosopher, I am told.

Sparsit   Indeed, sir, is she?

Harthouse   Excuse my impertinent curiosity. I am about to know the family, and may have much to do with them. Is the lady so very alarming? Her father gives her such a portentously hard-headed reputation – though she must be a little younger than her husband. Perhaps five and thirty?

Sparsit   A chit. Not twenty when she was married. Now twenty-one.

Harthouse   I give you my honour, Mrs Sparsit, that I never was so astonished in my life. I assure you that the father's manner prepared me for a grim and stony maturity. I am obliged to you, of all things for correcting so absurd a mistake.

Sparsit   The address of the Bounderby residence. (*Handing it over.*)

Harthouse   Many thanks. Pray excuse my intrusion. Good day.

Exit **Harthouse**.

Sparsit *moves to the window to watch* **Harthouse** *emerge into the street.*

Sparsit   James Harthouse! Good looking, good figure, good teeth, good voice, good breeding. Oh Mr Bounderby – you fool!

Scene Sixteen

Bounderby's Parlour

Louisa *by the fire.*

Enter **Bounderby**, *followed closely by* **Harthouse**.

Bounderby   Mr Harthouse, before assuring you of the
pleasure with which I shall respond to my friend Tom
Gradgrind's letter of introduction I have one thing to say to
you. You are a man of family. Don't you deceive yourself by
supposing for a moment that I am a man of family. I am a bit
of dirty riff-raff, and a genuine scrap of rag, tag and bobtail.

Harthouse   Assuredly, sir, nothing could exalt my interest
in you more than to hear of the circumstances of your birth
and upbringing.

Bounderby   So now we may shake hands on equal terms –
and I will introduce you to my wife. Here she is. Loo, Mr
James Harthouse.

Harthouse   How do you do, Mrs Bounderby.

Louisa   Good evening.

Bounderby   Loo, Mr Harthouse has joined your father's
muster-roll. You observe, Mr Harthouse, that my wife is my
junior. I don't know what she saw in me to marry me, but
she saw something in me, I suppose. She has lots of
expensive knowledge, sir, political and otherwise. If you
want to cram for anything, I should be troubled to
recommend you to a better adviser than Loo Bounderby.

Harthouse   I'm sure I could not be recommended to a
more agreeable adviser.

Bounderby   If you're in the complimentary line, you'll get
on here, for you'll meet with no competition.

Louisa   Mr Harthouse, are you going to devote yourself, as
my father has, to the service of your country? To show the
nation the way out of all its difficulties?

Harthouse   Mrs Bounderby, upon my honour, I will make no such pretence to you. I am going in for your respected father's opinions, because I have no choice of opinions, and may as well back them as anything else.

Louisa   You are a singular politician.

Harthouse   You are a singular lady.

Bounderby   I am Josiah Bounderby of Coketown, and that's enough for me.

Harthouse   As your father published you, a cool intellectual.

Enter **Tom**. **Louisa**'s *impassive face breaks into a beautiful smile.* **Harthouse** *is struck by this contrast and takes an immediate interest in* **Tom**.

Louisa   Tom! Where have you been all evening?

Bounderby   When I was your age, young Tom, I was punctual, or I got no dinner.

Tom   When you were my age, you hadn't a wrong balance to get right, and hadn't to dress afterwards.

Louisa   Tom, this is Mr Harthouse – a friend of Father's, from London.

Tom   How do you do, sir.

Bounderby   Tom works in my Bank. I'm bringing him on, so to speak.

Harthouse   Enchanted to meet you, Tom. Your face is quite familiar to me. Can I have seen you abroad?

Tom   No such luck, sir.

Bounderby   Coketown, sir, is not the kind of place you have been accustomed to. Therefore, if you will allow me – or whether you will not, for I am a plain man – I'll tell you something about it.

Harthouse   I would be charmed to hear.

Bounderby   First of all, you see our smoke. That's meat and drink to us. It's the healthiest thing in the world in all respects, and particularly for the lungs.

Tom   Is there any wine?

Louisa *serves* **Tom** *with wine.* **Harthouse** *watches her closely.*

Bounderby   Now, you have heard a lot of talk about the work in our mill, no doubt. I'll state the fact of it to you. It's the pleasantest work there is, and it's the lightest work there is, and it's the best-paid work there is.

Harthouse *observes* **Tom** *pulling faces at* **Bounderby**.

More than that, we couldn't improve the mills themselves, unless we laid down Turkey carpets on the floors, which we're not a-going to do.

Harthouse   Mr Bounderby, perfectly right.

Bounderby   Lastly, as to our Hands. There's not a Hand in this town, sir, man, woman or child, but has one ultimate object in life. That object is, to be fed on turtle soup and venison with a gold spoon.

Tom   What time's dinner?

Bounderby   Now, they are not a-going – none of 'em – ever to be fed on turtle soup and venison with a gold spoon. And now you know the place.

Harthouse   Oh yes. I am instructed to the highest degree, sir, on the whole Coketown question.

Drum roll – cymbal splash!

Enter **Sleary**, **Wild Huntsman**, *Clown*, **Snake Charmer**, *tom-tom rhythm – snake rattle. The Circus plays a dark snake-charming tune, as the* **Bounderby** *party rise and head into dinner.*

End of Act One

Interval

Act Two

Prologue

A Coketown Street

Smoke and steam – the piston of the steam engine, working monotonously up and down like the head of an elephant.

Company of Mill Hands enter – **Stephen Blackpool** *among them.*

They dance a clog chorus – the choreography of which highlights **Stephen***'s isolation.*

This dance may be to music (a reprise of The Four Loom Weaver) or rhythm only.

Scene One

Bounderby's Parlour

Bounderby, **Louisa**, **Tom** *and* **Harthouse**. **Stephen Blackpool** *standing.*

Bounderby   Well Stephen, what's this I hear? What have these pests of the earth been doing to you? Come in and speak up. This is the man I was telling you about, Harthouse.

Stephen   What were it, sir, as you were pleased to want wi' me?

Bounderby   Why I have told you. Tell us about yourself and this combination.

Stephen   Wi' your pardon, sir. I have nowt to say about it.

Bounderby   It's my understanding that these Union men have put a mark upon you.

Are you afraid to open your lips about them?

Stephen   I said as I had nowt to say.

Bounderby   Then you had better tell us at once, that the scoundrel Slackbridge is not in the town, stirring up the people to mutiny.

Stephen   I'm as sorry as you, sir, when the people's leaders is bad. Haply, 'tis not the smallest of their misfortunes.

Bounderby   Pray Mr Blackpool, may I take the liberty of asking you how it happens that you refused to be in this combination?

Stephen   I made a promise.

Bounderby   It is because you know that Slackbridge and his Union friends are a set of rascals and rebels whom transportation is too good for.

Stephen   Nay. They've not done me a kindness, but there's not one among but believes as he has done his duty by the rest and by himself. God forbid as I that have known o these men all my life, should fail to stand by em.

Bounderby   They have turned you adrift.

Stephen   I canna think the fault is all with us.

Bounderby   Indeed! Here's a gentleman from London present. A Parliament gentleman.

Stephen   Sir.

Bounderby   So tell him. What do you complain of?

Stephen   I have not come here, sir, to complain. I come for that I were sent for.

Bounderby   What do you people in a general way complain of?

Stephen   Look round town – so rich as tis – and see the numbers o' people as has been broughten into bein here for to weave, and to card and to piece out a living. Look how we live, from cradle to grave. Who can look on it, sir, and fairly tell a man 'tis not a muddle.

Bounderby   And how would you set this 'muddle' to rights? I'll tell you – by making an example of half a dozen Slackbridges. We'll ship the blackguards off to penal settlements.

Stephen   Sir, if you was t' tak a hundred Slackbridges, and sink em in the deepest ocean, you'd leave the muddle just where tis. Tis not by them the trouble's made. I canna with my little learning and my common way tell the gentlemen what will better all this – but I can tell him what I know.

As **Louisa** *is the only one in the room listening with any attention or understanding,* **Stephen** *gradually directs his speech to her . . .*

The strong hand will never do 't. Nor yet letting alone will never do it. Most of all, rating the workers as so much power, and regulating em as if they were as figures in a sum or machines, without loves and likens, memories and inclinations, without souls to weary or souls to hope, will never set this muddle to rights.

Bounderby   Stop a bit. I told you the last time you were here with a grievance that I was up to the gold spoon lookout. Now it's clear to me that you are one of those chaps who have always got a grievance.

Stephen *shakes his head.*

Bounderby   You are such an ill-conditioned chap that even your own Union will have nothing to do with you. I never thought those fellows could be right in anything; but I tell you what, I so far go along with them for a novelty, that I'll have nothing to do with you either. You can finish off what you're at, and then go elsewhere.

Stephen   Sir, you know well that if I canna get work wi' you, I canna get it elsewhere.

Bounderby   What I know, I know, and what you know, you know. I have no more to say about it.

Stephen *looks to* **Louisa**, *who cannot meet his eyes.*

Stephen   Heaven help us all in this world.

Scene Two

A Coketown Street

Stephen *steps out into the street.* **Rachael** *is waiting.*

Stephen   Rachael, my dear.

Rachael   What did he want?

Stephen   You shouldn't ha' come wi' me, Rachael. It might bring trouble on you.

Mrs Pegler *in the shadows.*

Pegler   Good evening.

Stephen   Who's there?

Pegler   Remember me? Here I am again. I heard of him being married. I read it in the paper – oh it looked fine.

Stephen   Rachael, this the lady I told you of. Who comes to see Mr Bounderby.

Pegler   I want to see his wife. I have never seen her yet. She hasn't come out of that house since noon today, but I was waiting a little last bit more.

Stephen   Well, missus. I have seen the lady and she were young and handsome.

Pegler   Young and handsome. Yes! And what a happy wife!

Stephen   Aye missus, I suppose she be.

Pegler   Suppose? She must be. She's your master's wife.

Stephen   Not master any more.

Rachael   Have you left his work, Stephen?

Stephen   Whether I have left his work, or whether his work has left me, comes to the same. Tis as well so – better, for you and me, Rachael.

Rachael   Where will you go?

Stephen   I dunno, but I'm not going tonight, Rachael. Nor yet tomorrow. T'aint easy to know where to turn, but a good heart will come to me.

Pegler   I must be on my way. You have seen Mrs Bounderby, and once more your eyes will have to serve for mine.

Stephen   Will you step into my place, missus, and take a cup o' tea before you go? If you come, so will Rachael. And afterwards I'll see thee safe t' thy traveller's lodging. It may be long, Rachael, ere ever I have th' chance o' thy company again.

Scene Three

Stephen's house

Enter **Stephen**, **Rachael** *and* **Mrs Pegler**.

Stephen   I have never thought yet, missus, o' asking thy name.

Pegler   Mrs Pegler. I'm a widow of many long years. He was a good husband – the best on record.

Stephen   Did you have any children?

Pegler   No. Not now. Not now.

Stephen   Not now?

Rachael *gives him a look.*

Stephen   Oh. I'm sorry I spoke on it.

Knock at the door. **Rachael** *goes to answer.*

Pegler   I had a son, and he did well – wonderfully well. But he is lost.

Rachael *returns.*

Rachael   It's Mrs Bounderby.

Pegler   Bounderby!

Rachael   Shall she come in?

Pegler   Oh, don't let me be seen. Don't let him come in till I've got away.

Rachael   No, not Mr Bounderby. Just his wife, and her brother.

Stephen   Hearken, missis. Tis Mrs Bounderby. You wanted to see her.

Pegler   You're sure it's the lady and not the man?

Rachael   Yes.

Stephen   Tell her come in.

Rachael *exits*.

Pegler   Pray, don't speak to me, nor yet take any notice of me.

Enter **Rachael** *with* **Louisa** *and* **Tom**.

Louisa   Mr Blackpool. I have come to speak to you in consequence of what passed just now. I should like to be serviceable to you, if you will let me. Is this your wife?

Rachael   !

Louisa   I remember. I have heard your domestic misfortunes spoken of. It was not my meaning to ask a question that would give pain to anyone here. (*To* **Rachael**.) He has told you what has passed between himself and my husband?

Rachael   I have heard the end of it, young lady.

Louisa   Did I understand that being rejected by one employer he would probably be rejected by all?

Rachael   The chances are next to nothing for a man who gets a bad name.

Louisa   He fell into suspicion with his fellow weavers because he had made a promise not to join the Union.

Rachael   I didn't seek it of him, poor lad.

Stephen   No one excepting myself can ever know what love and respect I bear to Rachael. When her little sister were killed in an accident I were all for stirring things up, but she begged me to 'let be'. So I swore I'd not fight the factory owners; not then, nor ever again. Twere a solemn promise.

Rachael   I prayed him to avoid trouble for his own good. But he'd die a hundred deaths ere ever he'd break is word.

Louisa   What will you do?

Stephen   Well, ma'am, when I have finished off, I must quit this part, and try another. There's nowt to be done without trying.

Louisa   How will you travel?

Stephen   On foot.

Louisa *takes out her purse and removes a note.*

Louisa   Rachael, will you tell him – for you know how, without offence – that this is freely his, to help him on his way?

Rachael   Bless you for thinking o' the lad wi' such tenderness. But tis for him to know his heart and what is right according to it.

Stephen   Not e'en Rachael could make such a kind offering, by any words, kinder. To show that I'm not a man without reason and gratitude, I'll take two pound. I'll borrow it for to pay it back.

Louisa *puts away the note and give* **Stephen** *two sovereigns.*

Louisa   And now I must go. Tom . . .

Tom   Just a moment, Loo. Something comes into my head. If you'll step out with me, Blackpool . . .

Stephen *follows* **Tom** *out of the room. We follow . . .*

Tom   When are you off?

Stephen   Today's Monday . . . why, sir, Friday or Saturday night about.

Tom   Friday or Saturday. Now look here. I am not sure that I can do you the good turn I want to do you, but I may be able to. So I tell you what – do you know the light porter at the Bank – his name is Bitzer?

Stephen   I know him by sight.

Tom   Very well. When you leave work on a night, between this and your going away, just hang about the Bank an hour or so, will you? And if I find I can do you the service I want to do you, Bitzer will have a note or message for you – but not else. Do you understand?

Stephen   I understand, sir.

Tom   Be sure you don't make any mistake then, and don't forget. Very well then. Come along, Loo!

Tom *and* **Louisa** *exit to the street.* **Stephen** *returns to the room.*

Pegler   Mrs Bounderby. A pretty wife. I shall weep for joy. Very fine eyes, I do declare. And clever. Oh yes. I see that too. What a happy wife she must be.

Stephen *and* **Rachael** *look at each other.*

Scene Four

A Coketown tavern

Tom *and company have been drinking and gaming all night.* **Harthouse** *looks on – sober.*

Tom (*Sings.*)
    There lives a lad in the old north country
    As bright and bold as any man might be
    His hands are quick, and his heart is free
    And they call him the merry juggler

Fiddle-eye-o! Fiddle-eye-ay!
He's a juggler all the day
He's a juggler all the day

This clever lad, he plays a winning game
At cards and dice he has found fame
And at the table he has another name
For they call him the merry gambler

Fiddle-eye-riddle-eye-o! Fiddle-eye-riddle-eye-ay!
He's a gambler all the day
He's a gambler all the day

What does the gambler and the juggler do
When the play is past and the day is through
Why he then likes to take a glass or two
So they call him the merry tippler

(*Faster.*)

Fiddle-eye-riddle-eye-tipple-eye-o! Fiddle-eye-riddle-eye-
tipple-eye-ay!
He's a tippler all the day
He's a tippler all the day

Fiddle-eye-riddle-eye-tipple-eye-o! Fiddle-eye-riddle-eye-
tipple-eye-ay!
He's a tippler all the day
He's a tippler all the day

Laughter and cheers for **Tom**, *and the company disperses.*

Tom   Your good health, Mr Harthouse.

Harthouse   Please, call me Jem.

Tom *lifts his glass and takes another drink.*

Tom   Jem!

Harthouse   You surprise me, Tom. I understood there was
a leaning to Temperance in these towns, and among the
hard fact men.

Tom   Do I look like a hard fact man to you?

Harthouse *lifts his own glass.*

Harthouse   Your very good health.

Tom   You'll have had about a dose of old Bounderby these past few nights.

Harthouse   An excellent fellow indeed.

Tom   You think so, don't you?

Harthouse   What a comical brother-in-law you are, Tom!

Tom   Oh, I don't care for old Bounderby and I have always thought of him in the same way. I am not going to begin to be polite now.

Harthouse   Don't mind me, but take care when his wife is by.

Tom   His wife? Oh yes! My sister Loo never cared for old Bounderby either.

Harthouse   That's the past tense, Tom. We are in the present tense now.

Tom   Verb neuter, not to care. Indicative mood, present tense. First person singular, I do not care; second person singular, thou dost not care; third person singular, she does not care.

Harthouse   You don't mean it.

Tom   Upon my honour. Why, you won't tell me, Mr Harthouse, that you really suppose my sister Loo does care for old Bounderby.

Harthouse   My dear fellow, what am I bound to suppose, when I find two married people living in harmony and happiness?

Tom   You know our father, Mr Harthouse, and therefore you needn't be surprised that Loo married old Bounderby. She never had a lover and the governor proposed old Bounderby and she took him.

Harthouse   Very dutiful in your interesting sister.

Tom   Yes, but she wouldn't have been as dutiful, and it would not have come off as easily if it hadn't been for me. I persuaded her. I was stuck into old Bounderby's Bank (where I never wanted to be) and I knew I should get into scrapes there if she put old Bounderby's pipe out; so I told her my wishes and she came into them. She would do anything for me. It was very game of her, wasn't it?

Harthouse   It was charming, Tom.

Tom   Not that it was altogether so important to her as it was to me, because my liberty and comfort depended on it, and she had no other lover, and staying at home was like staying in jail – especially when I was gone.

Harthouse   And she gets on so placidly.

Tom   She has settled down to the life, and she don't mind. Besides, though Loo is a girl, she's not a common sort of girl. She can shut herself up within herself, and think. I have often known her sit and watch the fire for an hour at a stretch.

Harthouse   She has resources of her own.

Tom   Not so much of that as you may suppose, for our governor had her crammed with all sorts of dry bones and sawdust. It's his system. He formed me that way too. When I first left home and went to old Bounderby's, I was as flat as a warming-pan, and knew no more about life than any oyster does.

Harthouse   Come, Tom, I can hardly believe that.

Tom   Upon my soul. Oh, I've picked up a little since I don't deny that. But I have done it myself; no thanks to the governor.

Harthouse *pours more whisky.*

Harthouse   And your intelligent sister?

Tom   She used to complain to me that she had nothing to fall back upon, that girls usually fall back upon – such as

music and stories. But she don't mind. Girls can always get
on somehow.

Harthouse   But you don't get on, Tom?

Tom   I would be better if she would help me more. She
married old Bounderby for my sake, so why doesn't she
make herself more agreeable to him and get me what I want,
instead of sitting in his company like a stone.

Harthouse   When I called at the Bank that first evening for
Mr Bounderby's address, I found an ancient lady there, who
seems to entertain great admiration for your sister.

Tom   You mean Mother Sparsit?

Harthouse   And that strange porter . . .

Tom   Bitzer! Her spy. He's a sly one. Watch out for him.
The two of them are like vultures, up in their room over the
Bank – watching for any sign of weakness in their fellow
creatures below.

Harthouse   Weakness?

Tom   They never miss a thing.

Harthouse   Is that so?

Tom   I'm betting on it.

Music.

All (*Sing.*)
    Fiddle-eye-riddle-eye-tipple-eye-o! Fiddle-eye-riddle-eye-
    tipple-eye-ay!
    He's a tippler all the day
    He's a tippler all the day

Scene Five

A Coketown Street

Evening, two days later. Thunder.

Stephen Blackpool *stands in the street opposite the Bank, with a bundle at his feet.* **Rachael** *approaches.*

Rachael   Stephen! What dost tha do here?

Stephen   I'm waiting for some help – though I don't know what, and none has come.

Rachael   I thought tha'd gone. Thy loom is empty.

Stephen   I should have tried to see thee again, Rachael, afore I go. My work was finished today. My bundle's made up.

Rachael   Thou wilt write to me, Stephen?

Stephen   I will. But now thou must not speak to me more.

Rachael   May Heaven bless thee, Stephen, in all thy wanderings, and send thee peace and rest at last.

Rachael *moves to exit,* **Stephen** *calls after her.*

Stephen   I towd thee, my dear, that I would never see or think o' anything that angered me but thou, so much better than me, should'st be beside it. Thou'rt beside it now. Thou mak'st me see it wi a better eye. Bless thee. Good night. Goodbye.

Rachael *is gone.* **Stephen** *alone.*

Music – traditional tune: The Four Loom Weaver. (The tone is solemn.)

All (*Sing.*)
  I'm a four loom weaver as many a one knows
  I've nowt to eat and I've worn out me clothes
  Me clogs are both broken, and stockings I've none
  Tha'd scarce give me tuppence for a' I've gotten on.

Stephen Blackpool *picks up his bundle with sorrow, but no self-pity, and disappears into the night.*

Scene Six

Bounderby's garden.

Louisa *and* **Harthouse**.

Harthouse   Mrs Bounderby, I esteem it a most fortunate accident that I find you alone here. I have a particular wish to speak to you.

Louisa   On what matter, Mr Harthouse?

Harthouse   Your brother. My young friend Tom.

Louisa   Tom? (*A lovely smile.*) What of him? Mr Harthouse?

Harthouse   Pardon me. The expression of your sisterly interest is so beautiful . . .

Louisa   I am waiting for your further reference to my brother.

Harthouse   Your brother. I have an interest in him.

Louisa   Have you an interest in anything, Mr Harthouse?

Harthouse   If you had asked me when I first came here, I should have said no. I must say now – even at the hazard of appearing to make a pretence – yes.

Louisa   Mr Harthouse, I give you credit for being interested in my brother.

Harthouse   Thank you. Mrs Bounderby, it is no irrevocable offence in a young fellow of your brother's years if he is heedless, inconsiderate and expensive. Is he?

Louisa   Yes.

Harthouse   Allow me to be frank. Do you think he gambles at all?

Louisa (*Pause.*)   I know he does.

Harthouse   Of course, he loses.

Louisa   Yes.

Harthouse   May I hint at the probability of your sometimes supplying him with money for these purposes?

Louisa *looks at him.*

Harthouse   My dear Mrs Bounderby, I think Tom may be gradually falling into trouble. I doubt whether – forgive my plainness – whether there is any great confidence between Tom and his most worthy father?

Louisa   I do not think it likely.

Harthouse   Or between himself and his highly esteemed brother-in-law?

Louisa   I do not think that likely either.

Harthouse   Mrs Bounderby, may there be a better confidence between yourself and me? I think Tom has borrowed a considerable sum of you?

Louisa   Mr Harthouse, if I tell you what you press to know, it is not by way of complaint or regret.

Harthouse *nods his understanding.*

Louisa   When I married, I found that my brother was even at that time heavily in debt. Heavily enough to oblige me to sell some trinkets. They were no sacrifice. Since then I have given my brother, at various times, what money I could spare; in short, what money I have had. But, even since you arrived here he has wanted in one sum as much as a hundred pounds. I have not been able to give it to him. I have kept these secrets until now, I trust them to your honour.

Harthouse   Mrs Bounderby, I understand and share the wise consideration with which you regard your brother's errors, and I wish to stretch out a helping hand to him. However, I have one great fault to find with Tom which I cannot forgive.

Louisa   ?

Harthouse   I cannot forgive him for not being more sensible of the affection of his best friend, of her unselfishness and sacrifice.

Louisa   That is of no consequence, Mr Harthouse. But if you can help him . . .

Bounderby *bursts into the room.*

Bounderby   Harthouse, have you heard?

Harthouse   Heard what?

Bounderby   Then you haven't heard.

Harthouse   Heard what?

Bounderby   The Bank's been robbed. Robbed last night, sir. Robbed with a false key.

Harthouse   Of much?

Bounderby   Why, no, not of very much. But it might have been.

Harthouse   How much?

Bounderby   Oh, as a sum, of not more than a hundred and fifty pound. But it's not the sum, it's the fact. It's the fact of the Bank being robbed, that's the important circumstance. I am surprised you don't see it.

Harthouse   My dear Bounderby, I do see it. Nevertheless, I may be allowed, I hope, to congratulate you on your not having sustained a greater loss.

Bounderby   But I tell you what, it might have been twenty thousand pound.

Harthouse   I suppose it might.

Bounderby   Suppose it might! By George, it might have been twice twenty.

Mrs Sparsit *enters, having been incapable of keeping pace with her employer.*

Here's a lady knows pretty well what it might have been, if you don't. Dropped sir, as if she was shot when she heard the news.

Harthouse   How are you, Mrs Bounderby?

Bounderby   You know this lady (for she is a lady), Mrs Sparsit?

Harthouse   I have had the honour / . . .

Bounderby   Yesterday afternoon, at the close of business hours, everything was put away as usual. In the iron room that the light porter, Bitzer, sleeps outside of, there was – never mind how much. In the little safe in young Tom's closet, the safe used for petty purposes, there was a hundred and fifty odd pound. Sometime in the night, while this young Bitzer snored – Mrs Sparsit, ma'am, you say you heard him snore?

Sparsit   Sir, I cannot say that I have heard him precisely snore, but on winter evenings, when he has fallen asleep at his table, I have heard him, what I should prefer to describe as partially choke, and produce sounds of a nature similar to what may be sometimes heard in Dutch clocks / . . .

Bounderby   Well, while Bitzer was snoring, or choking or Dutch clocking – some fellows, somehow, got to young Tom's safe, forced it, and abstracted the contents. They then made off; letting themselves out at the main door, and double-locking it again with a false key, which was picked up in the street near the Bank.

Harthouse   Where is Tom, by the way?

Bounderby   He and Bitzer have been helping the police.

Harthouse   Is anybody suspected?

Bounderby   Suspected? I should thing there was somebody suspected. Egod. Josiah Bounderby of Coketown is not to be plundered and nobody suspected.

Harthouse Who is suspected?

Bounderby Now wait a bit. (*Wipes his forehead.*) What should you say to a Hand being in it?

Harthouse I hope, not our friend Blackpool.

Bounderby That's the man.

Louisa No!

Bounderby Yes! Show me a dissatisfied Hand and I'll show you a man that's fit for anything bad. You recall, Harthouse, what I said to him here in this very house? Three days after that, he bolted. Went off, nobody knows where. What did he do before he went? He was watching the Bank.

Night after night. Mrs Sparsit saw him, and Bitzer too. What do you say to that?

Harthouse Suspicious, certainly.

Bounderby But there are more of 'em in it. There's an old woman. An old woman who seems to have been flying into town on a broomstick every now and then, and who was seen going into Blackpool's house on the night you saw him here. She has also been observed by Mrs Sparsit and Bitzer watching the Bank.

Sparsit A most villainous face and delinquent demeanour. I should recognise her on the instant if I ever saw her again.

Bounderby Mrs Sparsit's nerves have been acted upon by this business,

Sparsit Thank you very much, sir. But pray do not let my comfort be a consideration. Anything will do for me.

Sparsit *takes* **Bounderby**'s *arm and they exit to the house.*

Harthouse *and* **Louisa** *exchange a look.* **Harthouse** *decides to make himself scarce and also exits.*

Enter **Tom**.

Louisa   Tom, you're back!

Tom   And not before time. How tedious policemen are.

Louisa   Tom, if ever you loved me in your life, and have anything concealed from everyone besides, tell it to me.

Tom   I don't know what you mean, Loo.

Louisa   You can tell me nothing that will change me. Oh, Tom, tell me the truth.

Tom   What is it you want to know?

Louisa   You may be certain that I will not reproach you. Only say yes, and I shall understand you. (*Pause*) Not a word, Tom.

Tom   How can I say 'Yes' when I don't know what you mean.

Louisa   Have you said to anyone that we made a visit to Stephen Blackpool?

Tom   No. You particularly asked me to keep it quiet.

Louisa   I did not know then what was going to happen.

Tom   Nor I. How could I?

Louisa   You remember that Rachael was there, and there was an old woman too – who hung back in the shadows and said nothing. Ought we to say that we saw them?

Tom   Say what you like.

Louisa   Tom, do you believe the man I gave that money to is implicated in this crime?

Tom   I don't see why he shouldn't be.

Louisa   He seemed to me an honest man. What did you say to him, outside the door?

Tom   I told him that I thought he might consider himself very well off to get such a windfall as he had got from my sister, and that I hoped he would make good use of it.

Louisa   Was he offended by what you said?

Harthouse *reappears.* **Tom** *spots him over* **Louisa**'*s shoulder.*

Tom   I'm tired, Loo. I'll see you at dinner.

Exit **Tom**, *sulkily.* **Louisa** *covers her face. Music.*

Harthouse *approaches* **Louisa**, *with a parasol to shield her from the sun. He offers his arm to the trembling* **Louisa**.

Mrs Sparsit *appears, and watches them intently.* **Harthouse** *and* **Louisa** *slowly exit down the garden.* **Sparsit** *victorious.*

Sparsit   Oh, you fool!

Scene Seven

Mrs Gradgrind's room

Mrs G   Oh, my head!

Sissy   Let me bathe it for you.

Mrs G   Where are my children? Where are Tom and Louisa?

Sissy   We've sent for them.

Enter **Louisa**.

Mrs Bounderby is here.

Mrs G   Shhh. I never called him that. Not since he married Louisa.

Sissy   No, Mrs Bounderby is here.

Mrs G   Tell him to go away. He is a most alarming man. I never wanted him for her. It was all her father's doing. He set his heart on it.

Sissy   She doesn't know what she's saying.

Louisa   You needn't form an opinion on what she's saying.

Mrs G   Louisa? Is that you?

Louisa   Hello Mother.

Mrs G   Has that man gone – your husband?

Louisa   He was never here.

Mrs G   Tell him to go.

Louisa   He's gone, Mother.

Mrs G   Come closer, dear Louisa.

Louisa   Mother, why aren't you in bed?

Mrs G   I positively refuse to take to my bed. If I did, I'm sure I should never hear the last of it.

Sissy   She's very weak, Miss.

Mrs G   Well, my dear, and I hope you are going on satisfactorily to yourself.

Louisa   I want to hear of you, Mother, not of myself. Are you in pain?

Mrs G   I think there's a pain somewhere in the room, but I couldn't positively say that I have got it.

Louisa (*To* **Sissy**.)   Have you sent for my brother?

Sissy   Yes, though I don't know if he'll come.

Louisa   Of course he'll come.

Mrs G   Your father is almost always away now – in London. I must write to him about it.

Louisa   About what, Mother?

Mrs G   You must remember, my dear that whenever I have said anything on any subject I have never heard the last of it, and consequently I have long left off saying anything.

Louisa   What does she mean?

Mrs G   You learnt a great deal, Louisa, and so did you brother. Ologies of all kinds from morning to night. But there is something that your father has missed, or forgotten. I don't know what it is. I have often sat with Sissy near me, and thought about it. I shall never get its name now. But your father may. I want to write to him. To find out for God's sake what it is.

Sissy   We have sent for Mr Gradgrind also.

Mrs G   Give me a pen, give me a pen.

Louisa   Here, Mother.

Sissy *hands a pen to* **Louisa**, *but* **Mrs Gradgrind** *cannot take it. She sinks away and is gone.*

The two women stand in silence for a moment. **Sissy** *begins to cry, softly.*

Louisa, *dry eyed, picks up her mother's hand that has slipped to her side, kisses it and places it across the bosom of the body.*

Scene Eight

A graveyard

Music – a sad elegy, or hymn.

Mr Gradgrind, **Louisa**, **Sissy**, **Tom**, **Bounderby** *around a grave. Only* **Sissy** *showing any emotion.* **Sparsit** *at a respectable distance.* **Harthouse** *also hovering separately.*

The mourners break apart, moving away from the grave. **Sparsit** *steps forward to speak to* **Gradgrind**.

Sparsit   My condolences, Mr Gradgrind.

Gradgrind   Thank you, Mrs Sparsit.

Sparsit   Will you remain in Coketown for long?

Gradgrind   For the time being, yes.

Harthouse *has stepped forward to place a comforting hand on* **Louisa**'s *shoulder.*

Sparsit   Poor Louisa. She is quite downcast.

Gradgrind   Indeed.

Sparsit   Mr Harthouse is a great friend and comfort to her, as is her esteemed husband – of course.

Gradgrind   I have complete trust in her infinite good sense and lack of sentimentality. Her education has perfectly prepared her to endure sorrow without the torments that imagination may inflict upon the bereaved soul.

Bounderby   It's a pity the tumbling girl couldn't have been better taught not snivel like a ninny upon such occasions.

Gradgrind   I fear, she came to us too late.

Bounderby   Ah yes. All sorts of defects are found out in the stable door after the horse is stolen.

Gradgrind   Bounderby, have you received any intelligence respecting the robbery at the Bank?

At the question about the Bank, **Tom** *slopes away and off.*

Bounderby   Why no. I didn't expect it yet. Rome wasn't built in a day.

Sparsit   Very true.

Bounderby   Nor yet in a week, ma'am.

Sparsit   No, indeed, sir.

Gradgrind   Stephen Blackpool is not heard of?

Bounderby   Not as yet.

Gradgrind   Nor the old woman seen with him that night?

Gradgrind *and* **Bounderby** *move to exit.* **Sissy** *follows, still full of tears.*

Bounderby   She is not laid hold of either, but she will be. And I can wait. If Romulus and Remus could wait, Josiah Bounderby of Coketown can wait.

Gradgrind, **Bounderby** *and* **Sissy** *have now gone,* **Sparsit** *takes a last look round at* **Harthouse** *and* **Louisa**, *deep in private conversation, and exits.*

Louisa   You recollect the man, Mr Harthouse?

Harthouse   Oh, perfectly. And an infinitely dreary person he appeared to be.

Louisa   It has been very difficult for me to think ill of that man.

Harthouse   My dear Louisa, you know no good of the fellow.

Louisa   No, certainly. How can I?

Harthouse   Your Mr Blackpool was pulled up extremely short by Mr Bounderby. He was injured and left the house, where it appears he met with one who proposed to him some share in the Bank robbery.

Louisa   I feel as though it must be bad in me to be so ready to agree with you, and to be so lightened in my heart by what you say.

Harthouse   I have talked it over with my friend, your brother, more than once – and I remain on terms of perfect confidence with him.

Louisa   Thank you, Jem.

Harthouse   It is my pleasure only to see your face light up – and so beautifully.

He offers his arm and leads **Louisa** *away.*

Scene Nine

The room above the Bank

Sparsit *waiting, a silver supper salver and cloche, and glass of ale on the table. Enter* **Tom**.

Sparsit   Mr Thomas. I was hoping you'd come. Mr Bounderby being away on business, I thought you and I might review the day's proceedings in the Bank over a little supper.

Tom   You did say lamb chop and walnut ketchup.

Sparsit *lifts the cloche.*

Sparsit   And a glass of India ale!

Tom   Thank'ee Mrs Sparsit.

Sparsit   Is all shut up below, Tom?

Tom   Bitzer is attending to it. If he'd been more attentive a few weeks ago then perhaps the Bank would not have been robbed.

Sparsit   Indeed. And is there still no news of the suspect, Stephen Blackpool?

Tom   He's gone for good and all.

Sparsit   And how is your dear sister?

Tom *shrugs, eating.*

Sparsit   And what of Mr Harthouse?

Tom *shrugs again.*

Sparsit   Where has he been of late?

Tom   Shooting in Yorkshire. Sent Loo a basket half as big as a church last week.

Sparsit   The kind of gentleman whom one might wager to be a good shot.

Tom   Crack.

Sparsit   He's a great favourite of mine. May we expect to see him again shortly?

Tom   As a matter of fact I expected to see him tonight.

Sparsit You did?

Tom We were supposed to have dinner together. I went to meet him at the station, but he didn't appear. It's as well you'd invited me to supper, or I might have starved.

Sparsit I wonder where Mr Harthouse could have got to?

Tom I expect he'll turn up on the first train tomorrow. Excellent ale.

Sparsit – *galvanised.*

Sparsit Would you excuse me. I am suddenly faint and overcome. Bitzer will look after you. Enjoy your chop.

Sparsit *exits at speed.*

Scene Ten

Bounderby's garden (night)

Harthouse *earnestly wooing* **Louisa**.

Harthouse My dearest love. What could I do? Knowing your husband was away, was it possible I could miss the chance to be alone with you?

Louisa Please, Jem. You must go.

Harthouse Will you not bear my society a little while?

Louisa Not here.

Harthouse Where, Louisa?

Louisa Not here.

Sparsit *pops up, eavesdropping.*

Harthouse But we have so little time. Your brother could be home any moment.

Sparsit Ha!

Harthouse I have come so far, and I am so devoted.

Louisa   Please / . . .

Harthouse   I love you. You are the stake for which I desire to play away all I have in life. My darling Louisa, come away. Come away with me tonight.

Louisa   Oh, Jem.

Sparsit   Oh, you fool.

Drum roll.

Harthouse *leans forward and whispers urgently in* **Louisa**'s *ear.*

Louisa *nods and he, satisfied, exits hurriedly; passing the hidden* **Sparsit** *as he goes.* **Louisa** *stands, in a great dilemma.*

Cymbal splash! Music – Circus!

Enter **Sleary**, *and other Circus people. One carries a lit fire-eater's wand.*

Sleary   Hurry ladies. Hurry gentlemen – to see Louisa Bounderby, the world-famous fire-eater!

Louisa *is transfixed by the flame – looking for answers within it.*

Will she swallow the flames, or will the fire consume her? Who can tell? Her father has filled her with dry bones and sawdust. Perfect kindling! Hurry, hurry, for a ringside seat at this spectacular conflagration!

The fire wand draws **Louisa** *away, and off.* **Sleary** *close, in* **Sparsit**'s *ear . . .*

You don't wanna miss this one, missus!

All (*Sing.*)   Run away, run away, run away with us tonight.

Sparsit *rises to go after* **Louisa**, *but is stopped by the appearance of another flame.*

Sparsit   Ah! There you are . . ..

More flames will appear around the stage one by one; flickering in the darkness, as **Sparsit** *speaks – following the flames.*

She will walk to the nearby station.

All (*Sing.*)   Run away, run away . . . (*Flame.*)

Sparsit   From there she will board the train to Coketown. She will be there ahead of him, if he is riding. Where will she wait for him? And where will they go together? Patience, we shall see . . .

All (*Sing.*)   Run away, run away . . . (*Flame.*)

Sparsit   She may rendezvous with him and his carriage. If he's not waiting for her, she'll travel alone to their assignation.

All (*Sing.*)   Run away, run away . . . (*Flame.*)

Sparsit   I will pick up another carriage and follow close behind. Unless she is to make a connecting train.

The flames now move.

Sparsit *doesn't know which flame to pursue.*

Where is she? Where has she gone?

All the flames go out.

I have lost her. I have lost her.

Music ends. Blackout on **Sparsit***.*

The one true flame flickers in the fireplace of the **Gradgrind** *residence.*

Scene Eleven

Gradgrind's Parlour

Gradgrind*, seated reading. Enter* **Louisa***, greatly agitated.*

Louisa   Father!

Gradgrind   Louisa.

Louisa   Father, I want to speak to you.

Gradgrind   What is the matter? How strange you look.

Louisa   Father, you have trained me from my cradle.

Gradgrind   Yes, Louisa.

Louisa   I curse the hour in which I was born to such a destiny.

Gradgrind   Curse the hour?

Louisa   How could you give me life, and take from me all the things that raise it from the state of conscious death? Where are the graces of my soul? Where are the sentiments of my heart? Father – you remember the last time we conversed in this room?

Gradgrind   Yes, Louisa.

Louisa   What has risen to my lips now would have risen then if you had given me a moment's help. If you had known then what lingered in my breast, would you have given me to the husband whom I am now sure that I hate?

Gradgrind   No, no, my poor child.

Louisa   You proposed my husband to me. I took him. I never made a pretence to him or you that I loved him.

Gradgrind   I never knew you were unhappy, Louisa . . .

Louisa   Then chance threw into my way a new acquaintance; a man such as I had no experience of; worldly, polished, easy. He conveyed to me that he understood me, read my thoughts. There seemed to be a near affinity between us. I have not disgraced you. But if you ask me whether I have loved him or do love him I tell you plainly, Father, that it may be so. I don't know.

This night, my husband being away, he has been with me, declaring himself my lover. This minute he expects me, for I could not release myself from his presence any other way.

I do not know that I am sorry. I do not know that I am ashamed. All I know is your philosophy and your teaching will not save me. Now, Father, you have brought me to this. Save me by some other means.

Louisa *collapses sobbing in her father's arms.*

Sissy *enters, to take in the scene and meet* **Gradgrind***'s eyes. She sets her face in fierce love and resolve.*

Scene Twelve

Harthouse's room at the tavern

Music.

Harthouse *pouring himself a drink. A knock.*

Harthouse   Come in my darling.

Enter **Sissy***.*

Music cuts out suddenly.

Sissy   I speak to Mr Harthouse?

Harthouse   To Mr Harthouse. And you speak to him with the most confiding eyes I ever saw . . .

Sissy   I do not, sir. (*Pause.*) I think, you might guess whom I have left just now.

Harthouse   I have been in the greatest uneasiness during the last few hours, on a lady's account. You come from that lady, I trust?

Sissy   I do.

Harthouse   And where is she?

Sissy   At her father's.

Harthouse   Ah.

Sissy   She arrived there in great agitation. I have tended her in her distress. You may be sure, sir, you will never see her again as long as you live.

Harthouse   You are charged to convey that information to me by the lady herself?

Sissy   I have no charge from her.

Harthouse   Then there is yet hope.

Sissy   There is not the least hope.

Harthouse   But you said you had no commission from her.

Sissy   I have only the commission of my love for her, and her love for me. I have no other trust than that I know something of her character and her marriage. Oh, Mr Harthouse, I think you had that trust too.

Harthouse   I assure you that I had no particularly evil intentions.

Sissy   Then the only reparation that remains with you is to leave this town tonight, under an obligation never to return.

Harthouse   That is absurd. It would make a man ridiculous, after going in for these hard fact fellows, to back out in such an incomprehensible way.

Sissy   I am quite sure this is the only reparation in your power.

Harthouse   If I were to leave immediately – it would be in confidence.

Sissy   I will trust to you sir, and you will trust to me.

Harthouse   I suppose I must engage to do it.

Sissy   Yes, sir. Good evening, Mr Harthouse.

Harthouse   Wait. You have vanquished me at all points. Will you at least allow me the privilege of remembering my enemy's name?

Sissy   Sissy Jupe.

Harthouse   Of what family?

Sissy   I'm only a poor girl. My father was a stroller.

Harthouse   Only a poor girl. Only a stroller's daughter . . . Thank you. I wanted this to complete the defeat. (*He picks up pen and paper to write a note.*) Before you go, would you be so good as to send a telegram for me – to my brother in London . . . (*Hands the note to* **Sissy**.)

Sissy (*Reads.*)   Dear Jack, All up at Coketown. Bored out of the place, and going in for camels. Camels?

Harthouse   Camels.

Scene Thirteen

Gradgrind's Parlour

Gradgrind *alone.*

Bounderby *bursts in, with* **Mrs Sparsit**.

Bounderby   Now Tom Gradgrind, here's a lady here – Mrs Sparsit – you know Mrs Sparsit – who has something to say that will strike you dumb.

Gradgrind   You have missed my letter!

Bounderby   The present time is not time for letters. No man shall talk to Josiah Bounderby of Coketown about letters, with his mind in the state it's in now.

Gradgrind   Bounderby, I speak of a very special letter I have written to you in reference to Louisa.

Bounderby   Tom Gradgrind, I speak of a very special messenger that has come to me in reference to Louisa. Mrs Sparsit, ma'am, stand forward.

Mrs Sparsit *clears her throat in preparation for her moment of triumph – too many times for* **Mr Bounderby**.

If you can't get it out, ma'am, leave me to get it out. This is not a time for a lady, however highly connected, to be seemingly swallowing marbles. Tom Gradgrind, Mrs Sparsit latterly found herself in a situation to overhear a conversation out of doors between your daughter and your precious gentleman friend, Mr James Harthouse.

Gradgrind   Indeed.

Bounderby   And in that conversation / . . .

Gradgrind   It is not necessary to repeat its tenor, Bounderby. I know what passed.

Bounderby   You do? Perhaps you know where your daughter is at the present time!

Gradgrind   She is here.

Bounderby   !

Gradgrind   My dear Bounderby, the moment Louisa could detach herself from that interview with the person of whom you speak, she hurried here for protection. She presented herself before me in a state of distraction and has remained here ever since.

Pause. **Bounderby** *turns his outrage on* **Sparsit**.

Bounderby   Now ma'am! We shall be happy to hear any little apology you may think proper to offer, for going about the country at express pace, with no other luggage than a cock-and-a-bull, ma'am.

Sparsit   Sir, my nerves are at present too much shaken to admit of my doing nothing more than taking refuge in tears.

Bounderby   There is something else in which you may take refuge, namely, a coach. And the coach in which we came here being at the door, you'll allow me to hand you down to it, and pack you home to the Bank.

Bounderby *all but shoves the weeping* **Sparsit** *out of the door, and turns back to* **Gradgrind**.

Gradgrind   My dear Bounderby / . . .

Bounderby   Now, you'll excuse me, Tom Gradgrind, but I don't want to be too dear.

I am Josiah Bounderby of Coketown / . . .

Gradgrind   Bounderby, I see reason to doubt whether we have quite understood Louisa.

Bounderby   Who do you mean by 'we'?

Gradgrind   I doubt I have been quite right in the manner of her education.

Bounderby   There I agree with you.

Gradgrind   In the course of a few hours I have become better informed as to Louisa's character than in previous years. I think there are qualities in Louisa which – which have been harshly neglected, and – and if you would kindly meet me in a timely endeavour to leave her to her better nature for a while / . . .

Bounderby   You'd like to keep her here for a time?

Gradgrind   I – I recommend that you allow Louisa to remain here on a visit and be attended by Sissy (I mean Cecilia Jupe) who understands her and in whom she trusts.

Bounderby   You are of the opinion that there is what people call some incompatibility between Loo Bounderby and myself?

Gradgrind   I fear there is a general incompatibility between Louisa and – and – and almost all the relations in which I have placed her.

Bounderby   Now look here, Tom Gradgrind – I give you to understand, in reply to that, that there unquestionably is an incompatibility of the first magnitude – to be summed up in this – that your daughter don't properly know her husband's merits!

Gradgrind   Bounderby, I hoped you would have taken a different tone.

Bounderby   Highly connected females have been astonished to see the way in which your daughter has conducted herself, and have wondered how I have suffered it.

Gradgrind   Is it asking too much that you, so far her elder, should aid in trying to set her right? You have accepted a great charge of her; for better for worse / . . .

Bounderby   Come! I don't want to be told about that. I know what I took her for. And I am going to finish this business according to my own opinions. Now – your daughter, whom I made Loo Bounderby, and might have done better by leaving Loo Gradgrind, if she don't come home tomorrow, by twelve o'clock at noon, I shall understand that she prefers to stay away, and I shall send her wearing apparel and so forth over here, and you'll take charge of her for the future.

Gradgrind   Let me entreat you to reconsider / . . .

Bounderby   Whatever I do, I do at once. I have given you my decision, and I have got no more to say. Good night!

Scene Fourteen

A Coketown Street

Music.

Enter the 'Hands'.

Enter **Slackbridge**, *holding a handbill which reads 'TWENTY POUNDS REWARD FOR THE APPREHENSION OF STEPHEN BLACKPOOL'.*

Rachael *is conspicuously at the back, listening in sorrow and disbelief.*

Slackbridge Friends, behold of what a traitor in the camp is capable! Oh, my brothers and sisters, what do you say now of Stephen Blackpool, set forth in this degrading and disgusting document? Twenty pounds reward for the apprehension of the man suspected of complicity in the robbery of Coketown Bank. You remember how he stood here before you on this platform? You remember how he sidled and splitted of straws? You remember how I hurled him out from among us? Now he stands before us in all his native form – a thief, a plunderer, a fugitive!

Rachael *turns and leaves, hurriedly.*

But, my band of brothers, I propose to you that the community of Coketown Hands, having already solemnly disowned Stephen Blackpool, are free from the shame of his misdeed, and cannot be reproached with his dishonest actions.

Scene Fifteen

Gradgrind's Parlour

Louisa *and* **Gradgrind** *seated.*

Sissy, *standing, having just brought in* **Bounderby**, **Tom** *and* **Rachael**.

Bounderby   Tom Gradgrind, I don't disturb you, I hope, but here is a young woman who has been making statements. And as your son refuses for some obstinate reason to say anything at all about those statements, I am obliged to confront her with your daughter.

Rachael (*To* **Louisa**.)   You have seen me once before, young lady.

Louisa   I have.

Rachael   Will you make it known where, and who was there?

Louisa   I went to the house where Stephen Blackpool lodged, on the night of his discharge from work, and I saw you there. Also an old woman who did not speak. My brother was with me.

Bounderby   Why couldn't you say so, young Tom?

Tom   I promised my sister I wouldn't. And besides, she tells her own story so precious well, what business had I to take it out of her mouth.

Rachael   Say, young lady, if you please, why you came to Stephen's that night.

Louisa   I felt compassion for him and wished to offer him assistance.

Rachael   Did you offer him a bank note?

Louisa   Yes, but he refused it, and would only take two pounds in gold.

Rachael   Stephen Blackpool is now named as a thief in public print all over this town. There has been a meeting tonight where he has been spoken of in the most shameful way. Stephen!

Louisa   I am very, very sorry.

Rachael   Oh young lady, I hope you may be, but I don't know.

Tom   You're a pretty article. You ought to be bundled out for not knowing how to behave yourself.

Rachael   I have written to Stephen by the post that went out this afternoon. He will be here, at furthest, in two days.

Louisa   I hope he will clear himself.

Rachael   You need have no fear of that, young lady.

Bounderby   Yet you refuse to tell where he is.

Rachael   He shall come back of his own accord, and shame his accusers.

Bounderby   Well, if he can be laid hold of any sooner, he shall have an earlier opportunity of clearing himself. I wish you good night all.

Exit **Bounderby**, *followed by* **Tom**.

Louisa   Rachael, you will not distrust me when you know me better.

Sissy   Did you tell Stephen in your letter that suspicion has fallen upon him because he was seen about the Bank at night?

Rachael   I did – though I don't know why he was there.

Louisa   You will let me know the moment you hear from him.

Sissy   I will call at your lodging tomorrow night for news.

Rachael   Thank you – though I doubt if he can be here so quickly.

Sissy   Then I'll come the next night too.

Sissy *shows* **Rachael** *out, and returns quickly.*

Gradgrind   Louisa, I don't know this man Blackpool – do you believe him to be implicated?

Louisa   I have believed it, Father, though with great difficulty. I do not believe it now.

Gradgrind   His appearance and manner, they are so honest?

Louisa   Very honest.

Gradgrind   Then I ask myself does the real culprit know of these accusations?

Where is he? Who is he?

Louisa *and* **Sissy** *look at each other.*

Scene Sixteen

The Bank (inside and out)

Bounderby, **Tom**, **Bitzer**.

Bitzer   I'm ready to shut up now, Mr Bounderby.

Bounderby   Carry on, Bitzer. Three days, and still no news of the scoundrel. It's tolerably clear to me that the mill girl's letter gave him warning to fly.

Tom   The messengers reported that Rachael's letter was delivered, and that Blackpool decamped that same hour.

Bitzer   You're certain he's the thief, Master Tom?

Tom   A pretty question! If not, where is he? And why has he not come back?

Bounderby   My mother never came back, and though she was a wicked woman, this man is a worse subject than my mother.

Enter **Sissy**.

Sissy   Mr Bounderby, sir. I'm come on behalf of Rachael to tell you that she has still not had any word from Stephen – though she is unfailing in her hope of him, and ready to stand by him as soon as he returns.

Mrs Sparsit *suddenly sprints through, from her vantage point upstairs, and out into the street, yelling . . .*

Sparsit   Let nobody touch her. She belongs to me.

Bounderby   Mrs Sparsit, ma'am, what's afoot?

Sparsit *in the street, grappling with* **Mrs Pegler** *– an undignified tussle.*

Sparsit   It's Providence! Come into the Bank or I shall drag you in.

Pegler   No, please! I must not.

Sparsit   Oh yes you will! What is your name?

Pegler   Mrs Pegler.

Sparsit (*Fixing* **Mrs Pegler** *in a headlock.*)   Oh, is it! I should think it is!

Bounderby, **Bitzer** *and* **Tom** *follow outside.*

Bounderby   What's the matter now, Mrs Sparsit, ma'am?

Sparsit   Sir, I was gazing out of my window just now when whom should I espy but the old woman I saw watching the bank on the night of the robbery – and on several other occasions previously. She says her name is Pegler – but we can believe that if we may.

Sparsit *thrusts* **Mrs Pegler** *forward, and* **Bounderby** *sees her clearly for the first time.*

Bounderby   What do you mean by this? I ask you, what do you mean by this Mrs Sparsit, ma'am?

Sparsit   Sir?

Bounderby   Why don't you mind your own business!

Pegler   My dear Josiah! I am not to blame. This lady grabbed me and would not let go.

Bounderby   Couldn't you knock her tooth out, or scratch her, or something?

Pegler   I have always lived quiet and secret, Josiah. I have never broken the condition once. I have admired you at a distance and never told anyone I was your mother.

Sparsit   Your mother! Well, I am surprised, madam, that in your old age you have the face to claim Mr Bounderby for your son, after your unnatural and inhuman treatment of him.

Pegler   Me unnatural? Never!

Sparsit   You don't call it unnatural to desert your own child in his infancy and leave him to the brutality of a drunken grandmother?

Pegler   I deserted my Josiah? My boy will give you to know that he come of parents that loved him as dear as the best could, and that after his beloved father died, his mother did everything in her power to help him out in life. He worked his own way forward to be rich and thriving, and he pensioned me on thirty pound a year, only making the condition that I was to keep down in my own part and not trouble him. And so I have, though I do like to lay my eyes on my pride and joy once in a while unbeknownst to him. And for shame on you to accuse me of being a bad mother, with my son standing there to tell you different.

Pause.

Bounderby   Mrs Sparsit, ma'am. I rather think you are cramped at the Bank. It appears to me that under my humble roof there's hardly opening enough for a lady of your genius in other people's business. Don't you think you might find some affairs elsewhere, ma'am, to interfere with?

Sparsit   It never occurred to me before, sir, but now you mention it, I should think it highly probable.

Bounderby   Then suppose you try, ma'am. Suppose you try.

Exit **Sparsit**.

Bounderby   I am not bound to give a lecture on my family affairs. Those who expect any explanation whatever upon that subject will be disappointed.

Bounderby *grabs* **Mrs Pegler** *by the arm and exits back into the Bank, followed by* **Bitzer**.

Sissy   Well!

A mill hand runs on.

Mill Hand   All hands to the Old Hell Shaft! He's found.

Voices (*Off.*)   Bring ropes and lanterns. He's found! He's at the bottom of the shaft.

Tom   Who is found? Who's at the bottom of the shaft?

Mill Hand   They found his hat first. It had his name in it.

Sissy   Who?

Tom   Who is it?

Mill Hand   Stephen Blackpool.

Scene Seventeen

The top of the Old Hell Shaft

Music – The Four Loom Weaver.

Two Mill Hands carry on stretcher bearing the broken body of
Stephen Blackpool.

Stephen   Rachael.

Mill Hand   She's been sent for, Stephen.

The stretcher is set down. Enter **Rachael**, *with* **Sissy**.

Rachael   Where is he?

Stephen   Rachael.

Rachael   Oh Stephen.

She takes his hand.

Stephen   Rachael my dear. Don't let go.

Rachael   Thou'rt in great pain, my own dear Stephen?

Stephen   I have been, dreadful and long, my dear, but not
now. Ah Rachael, all a muddle. From the first to last, a
muddle. I fell into the pit, but look Rachael! Look above!
That star ha shined upon me in my pain and trouble. I could
see it at the top o' the shaft every night as it fell dark and I
was down there. It shined into my mind. I looked at it and I
thought o' thee, Rachael, till the muddle cleared away.

Louisa *and* **Gradgrind** *enter, with* **Tom** *shuffling behind.*

When I got thy letter, I easily believed there was a wicked
plot betwixt the young lady and her brother. When I fell I
were in anger wi' her, but that star shinin on me helped me
see more clear . . .

Louisa I'm here, Stephen.

Stephen You have a father. Will you tak a message to him?

Louisa He's here, Stephen. Shall I bring him to you?

Stephen If you please.

Louisa *indicates to* **Gradgrind** *to approach, which he does and takes his daughter's hand.*

Sissy *sidles up to* **Tom** *and whispers in his ear.* **Tom** *slips away.*

Sir, you will clear me and mak my name good wi all men. This I leave to you.

Gradgrind How, Stephen?

Stephen Your son will tell you how. Ask him. I mak no charges. I saw and spoke with your son one night. I ask no more o' you than that you clear me.

And I trust to you to do it.

Lift me up now and let me go. Rachael, beloved lass, don't let go my hand. We may walk together tonight, my dear.

Rachael I will hold thy hand and keep beside thee, Stephen, all the way.

Stephen Will somebody be pleased to cover my face.

Stephen *is lifted on the stretcher and carried off.*

Funeral bell.

When **Stephen** *has gone* **Gradgrind** *and* **Louisa** *remain, still holding hands.* **Sissy** *standing at a distance.*

Gradgrind Your wretched brother is already gone.

Louisa He will not come back to town tonight.

Gradgrind Do you think he had already planned this robbery when he went with you to Stephen's lodging?

Louisa   I know he wanted money very much and had spent a great deal.

Gradgrind   And it came into his evil brain to cast suspicion on this poor man about to leave town.

Louisa   I fear he somehow induced Stephen Blackpool to wait about the Bank those two or three nights before he left.

Gradgrind   And now, how is he to be saved from justice? In the few hours that I can allow to elapse before I publish the truth, how is he to be found by us and only by us?

Sissy   Forgive me, Mr Gradgrind. I know where he has gone.

Gradgrind   You, Sissy? How can you know where he's run off to?

Sissy   Because I told him where to go.

Scene Eighteen

The Circus

Outside the tent. Music.

Enter **Mr Sleary**.

Sleary   Ladies and Gentlemen and children – Sleary's Horse-riding is in town – bringing you the slack wire, the tight rope, knife-throwers, jugglers, acrobatics, fire-eaters – the Human Pyramid – all on bareback steeds!

Hurry – to see the daring Wild Huntsman of the North American Prairies.

All (*Sing.*)   Let the doyen of equestrian arts lighten your burden and gladden your hearts.

Sleary (*Spoken.*)   Marvel as the Emperor of Japan astride a white horse, twirls five wash-stand basins at once.

All (*Sing.*)   Brave and daring!

Sleary (*Spoken.*)   Hurry, as Miss Josephine Sleary will inaugurate the entertainments with her graceful Equestrian Tyrolean flower act.

All (*Sing.*)   Fearless, flaring!

Sleary (*Spoken.*)   Step this way for pleasing, but always strictly moral, wonders which must be seen to be believed.

All (*Sing.*)   Run away, run away, run away with us tonight.

Enter **Sissy** *and* **Louisa***, in travelling clothes.*

Sissy   Mr Sleary!

Sleary   Cecilia? Is that you?

They embrace with warmth and ease. **Louisa** *stands apart, uncertain.*

Why, it does me good to see you! You was always a favourite with us. You must see our people, or they'll break their hearts.

Sissy   But we must deal with the urgent business first, Mr Sleary.

Sleary   Of course, Cecilia. (*Lowering his voice.*) Now I don't ask to know any secrets, but I suppose this young lady is the sister?

Sissy   Yes.

Louisa   My father will be here shortly.

Sleary   I remember the Squire. I hope he is well.

Louisa   Is my brother safe?

Sleary   He is. He has the perfect disguise.

Louisa   Thank you, Mr Sleary. With all my heart. Thank you.

Enter **Gradgrind***.*

Sleary   Ah – there you are, Squire. Cecilia, will you go and kiss all our company, and send our new clown round this way.

Sissy *nods and exits.*

Gradgrind   I am indebted to you, Mr Sleary.

Sleary   All I say, Squire, is you stood by Cecilia, and I'll stand by you.

Enter **Tom** *– dressed as a clown.*

Louisa   Tom!

Tom *won't be embraced. He is sulky, ungrateful and humiliated.*

Sleary   I don't want to know what your son has been up to; it's better for me not to know. So I will leave you to your private affairs.

Sleary *exits.*

Gradgrind   Tom. How has it come to this?

Tom   !

Gradgrind   How was it done?

Tom   How was what done?

Gradgrind   The robbery.

Tom   I didn't take the money all at once. I pretended to put my balance away every night, but I didn't. I forced the safe myself the previous night, and shut it up ajar before I went away. I'd had the key that was found made long before. I dropped it that morning, that it might be supposed to have been used.

Gradgrind   If a thunderbolt had fallen on me, it would not have shocked me more than this.

Tom   I don't see why. So many people are employed in situations of trust; so many people, out of so many, will be dishonest. I have heard you talk, a hundred times, of its being a law. How can I help laws?

Gradgrind   You must be sent abroad.

Tom   I suppose I must.

Gradgrind (*Calls.*)   Mr Sleary!

Mr Sleary *appears.*

Sleary   Squire?

Gradgrind   How do we get this deplorable object away to a ship bound for America?

Sleary   Why I've been thinking of it, Squire. It's over twenty miles to the rail, but there he may catch the mail train to Liverpool. I offer a swift horse, and the Wild Huntsman of the North American Prairies to be his escort.

Gradgrind   Then I commend my son to your care, Mr Sleary. (*Hands* **Tom** *an envelope.*) Tom – all necessary means will be provided for you. Atone by repentance and better conduct, for the shocking action you have committed and the dreadful consequences to which it has led. Give me your hand, my poor boy, and may God forgive you as I do.

Tom   (*Shaking hands, with emotion*) Thank you, Father. (**Louisa** *steps forward to embrace him and his tone hardens.*) Not you. I don't have anything to say to you.

Louisa   Oh Tom, do we end so, after all my love?

Tom   After all your love? Leaving old Bounderby to himself, and packing my best friend Harthouse off, just when I was in the greatest danger.

Coming out with every word about our having gone to see Blackpool, when you saw the net was gathering round me. Pretty love that! You have regularly given me up. You never cared for me.

Sleary   Sharp's the word. Let's go!

Tom *and* **Sleary** *find their way barred by the sudden entrance of* **Bitzer**.

Bitzer   I'm very sorry to interfere with your plans, but young Mr Tom mustn't be got away by horse-riders. Here he is in motley and I must have him.

Gradgrind   Bitzer! Have you a heart?

Bitzer   No man, sir, acquainted with the facts relating to the circulation of the blood can doubt that I have a heart.

Gradgrind   Is it accessible to any compassionate influence?

Bitzer   It is accessible to reason, sir. And to nothing else. I suspected young Mr Tom of this bank robbery from the first. I had my eye upon him. I had the pleasure of watching your house yesterday morning and following you here. I am going to take young Mr Tom back to Coketown, sir. I have no doubt whatever that Mr Bounderby will then promote me to young Mr Tom's situation. And I wish to have his situation, sir, for it will be a rise to me.

Gradgrind   What sum of money will you set against your expected promotion?

Bitzer   Thank you, sir, but I find that to compound a felony, even on very high terms, would not be as safe and good for me as my improved prospects at the Bank.

Sleary   Squire, until this moment I didn't know what your son had done, and I didn't want to know – though I only thought it was some skylarking.

However, this young man having made it known to be a robbery of a bank, why that's much too serious a thing for me to compound.

Consequently, Squire, there's no help for you here. (*To* **Bitzer**.) Young sir, if you'll give us leave to finish our performance for the evening, I will escort you to the train station myself.

Bitzer   That is very reasonable of you, sir. Carry on with your performance.

Sleary   We will. Oh, we will!

Sleary *lifts a whistle to his lips and blows. Music – The Merry Juggler reprise.*

Strong Man, Snake Charmer, Wild Huntsman, Josephine Sleary *and* **Sissy** *all enter at a run.*

All (*Sing*)
> There lives a lad in the old north country
> As bright and bold as any man might be
> His hands are quick, and his heart is free
> And they call him the merry juggler
>
> Fiddle-eye-o! Fiddle-eye-ay!
> He's a juggler all the day
> He's a juggler all the day

A slapstick clowning / juggling routine, during which **Bitzer** *is overwhelmed. (This may variously include the Strongman rolling his dumbbell and knocking* **Bitzer** *off his feet; Snakes;* **Sissy** *tumbling and crashing into him; a pie in the face, or a bucket over the head)* **Sleary** *assisting, and apologising profusely throughout.*

Bitzer *is beaten.*

Tom *escapes with the* **Wild Huntsman**.

> Fiddle-eye-riddle-eye-tipple-eye-o! Fiddle-eye-riddle-eye-tipple-eye-ay!
> He's a tumbler all the day
> He's a tumbler all the day

Bitzer *is bundled away by the circus people, leaving* **Gradgrind**, **Sissy** *and* **Louisa** *outside the tent.*

Pause.

Gradgrind   Louisa, Sissy . . . I am wondering . . .

Louisa   Father?

Gradgrind   Wondering how to make amends. There are broadsides in the street, exonerating the late Stephen

Blackpool and publishing the guilt of my son. But how much more should be done – to bend my theories to appointed circumstances? To make facts and figures subservient to faith?

Louisa   And I wonder how Tom will fare, so far away from us all. I'm afraid he will never return.

Sissy   I believe that you will make amends, Mr Gradgrind. And I know that Tom's repentant heart is filled with love for his sister.

Louisa   And shall we leave you here now, Sissy, with your own people?

Sissy   No, Louisa. I'll stay with you – until you marry again.

Louisa   I will not marry again.

Sissy   Then I hope that I shall marry, and have children. Happy children. And they shall love you.

Louisa   And we shall think no innocent and pretty fancy ever to be despised.

Gradgrind   Then we shall sit with lighter bosoms on the hearth, to see the ashes of our fires turn grey and cold.

Mr Sleary *enters, with the Circus people shadowed behind him.* **Gradgrind** *reaches in his pocket for a penny. He pays* **Mr Sleary** *and enters the tent.*

Mr Sleary   People must be amused, somehow. They can't be always a working, nor a learning. I lay down the philosophy on the subject when I say to you, make the best of us, not the worst.

Music:

(*Sings.*)
   To the edges of the town
   Come the juggler and the clown
   Here the Wild Huntsman will give you a thrill
   Riding and shooting with breathtaking skill

All   Brave and daring! (*gasp*) Trapeze and wire!
Strength and might, all for your delight.
Fearless, flaring! Rattlesnake and fire!
Run away, run away, run away with us tonight.

THE END